From the House by the SEASHORE

Pati Adams

WESTBOW
PRESS®
A DIVISION OF THOMAS NELSON
& ZONDERVAN

WestBow Press books may be ordered through booksellers or by contacting:

WestBow Press
A Division of Thomas Nelson & Zondervan
1663 Liberty Drive
Bloomington, IN 47403
www.westbowpress.com
1 (866) 928-1240

ISBN: 978-1-4908-8531-5 (sc)
ISBN: 978-1-4908-8533-9 (hc)
ISBN: 978-1-4908-8532-2 (e)

Library of Congress Control Number: 2015909832

Print information available on the last page.

WestBow Press rev. date: 11/3/2015

To my 3 precious children in Heaven
Ryan, Stephanie and Timothy

My arms have never touched
My eyes have never seen
But my heart has always loved.

CONTENTS

I

NOW IT'S TWO, NOW IT'S BRACES, NOW WHAT?

New England is a very pretty place to start one's life. From a town call New Haven where some of its roots date back to 1640's and a University---called----Yale---that looks like it was dropped from London, England itself we take a small ride along this coastal region to where we will find a small town along the coast of Connecticut.

This town called Milford, has 14 miles of shoreline, was settle in 1639, showcases old restored homes and a river called Wepawaug that runs through part of the town. There is a town hall with its beautiful white pillars set against a duck pond and cascading waterfalls. On the other side of the duck pond is a magnificent structure----a tall white church with a steeple reaching to touch the sky. Also nudging along the duck pond we find another structure----Milford High School.

This is my town and this is where my story begins.

I lived with my mom and dad in a little house along the seashore of Milford, Connecticut. I had many hopes and dreams of becoming someone beautiful and that someday my prince would ride up on his white horse to carry me away to a beautiful land.

One day my mom and dad told me I was going to have a brother or sister. I was so excited, I told all my friends. I played in my yard with my friends, looked at the beautiful sky and wondered who created the sky with those white puffy clouds. I remember the day Mom had to go the hospital and, instead of one baby, they came home with two! At first I was happy, but then I noticed that I was not the only one anymore. Now I had to share my stuff with them!

As we grew up we'd take wonderful vacations to Cape Cod. We got along well, laughing, playing in the dunes, and just having a great time. I remember the smell of seafood, salt water and the cry of seagulls. It was the best time ever. My parents loved to take rides in the car. Problem number one was three kids and only two back windows. Sometimes I'd race to get a window seat and sometimes I didn't get it.

The brother who got stuck in the middle of the back seat during family road trips would keep touching my shoulders or leaning on me and sitting on top of me! Then he made fart noises or pretended he was going to pinch me. I'd yell at him to stop and tell my parents. But they said that all too famous line that every older kid knows, "You're the oldest, you should show them how to act right."

Act right! I couldn't even a get a word in edgewise with the two of them yacking the whole time. Then they'd tell Mom and Dad I was picking on them. And guess who they believed? Oh yes, the two little angel boys!! I'd just sit there with my arms crossed and gave them the evil eye, then stick out my tongue.

Then they'd whine, "Mommy, she's sticking her tongue out at us." Then I'd get in trouble. I'd smack both of them. Then the long arm of Dad appeared from the front seat and it was me who'd get smacked!

Oh yeah, I loved riding in the car! But I never failed to get the boys back. My parents had a can opener that looked like a big bumblebee. I found out Robert was deathly afraid of it. Every time my brother would come into the kitchen, I'd say, "Hey I am going to get the bug and it's going to get you!" He'd run away screaming and crying. I actually got pretty good at scaring him. I kept the bug can opener in my room—I felt more in control of any situation that may arise.

Saturdays in our house was "cleaning your room" day, before we could go out to play. When I was done with my room, I hit the back door to go out. My other brother Tony always hit my room and messed it up. He didn't like me scaring Robert with the bug can opener. So, the fighting began!

I remember on Sundays Dad would take us to church. Mom would go to an earlier service and have breakfast ready when we got home. One Sunday we were leaving church as usual, with the three of us in the back seat. Dad was driving through the parking lot and the back passenger door flew open and Tony fell out. Robert and I were glued to the back window crying and screaming to our dad that Tony just fell out of the car! He pulled over to get him and then walked him back to the car. Tony was crying and had a few cuts and bruises, but looked okay. That was the day I started trying to be nice to my brothers.

Sometimes during the year we'd go to Savin Rock in West Haven for a family night of hot dogs, French fries and chocolate milk. The real big treat was after dinner, the time to ride the huge merry-go-round on the beach. I always tried to catch that brass ring, but just never could do it.

When I was in third grade, my dad took me out of public school and put me into private school. When my brothers got older, they went to school with me. I remember our mom and dad saying they wanted us to have a good education. That was when they started to take God out of the public schools.

When I entered 5th grade my body started to change. I remember one time raising my hand—I wasn't feeling so good and needed to go the girls' room. The teacher told me I had to wait until lunchtime, but then realized the pain I was in. She brought me to the nurse's office and they called Mom. When we got home, she tucked me into bed.

My mom sat at the end of the bed and told me my body would start to change, then I saw her cry. I told her I liked the way it was before and I didn't like this change. I really did not like to see her crying either. A few weeks later, my body did start to change. I looked different and felt different. My face was changing, too, and I didn't like this at all. I had red marks on my face, my teeth started to stick out and I just felt skinny and ugly. I wondered what happened to that little girl who went to school a few weeks ago—and oh! I wanted her back. My mom said, "My little girl is now becoming a woman."

"Woman!?" Oh how I cried that night, asking God why this had to happen.

Three years later, in eighth grade and one of my so-called friends gave me letters from a boy that seemed to be interested in me. She brought letters from the boy. I read those letters and the wonderful things I was longing to hear. He said I was pretty, nice and wanted to ask me out on a date. My friend was the go-between. He actually gave me his I.D. bracelet and wanted to go steady. I was so thrilled. But the day came when I found out that my so-called friend and a bunch of other girls from my class were playing a cruel and mean trick on me. I found out that the boy was made up. I was not in their clique, so I was considered an outcast.

They thought the whole thing was pretty funny. So for the rest of my eighth grade year, I wanted to run and hide under a rock. This was supposed to be the best time in grade school, but it turned out to be a nightmare. I did not want to go to school any more. One day, I asked her why she did that to me. She told me "Because you are so dumb, easy and stupid, and nobody likes you anyway."

When I got home, I stayed in my bedroom and cried a lot. My mother asked me what was wrong. How could I tell my mother what some girls in school did to me? I felt so ashamed.

The first year of high school was very hard. There were some huge changes for me and I did not like them. I had buckteeth, skinny body and legs. I did not feel pretty anymore. I did make a few friends in my freshman year. A girl I grew up with, Samantha, and I always got along great. Samantha never laughed at me---she was always kind to me. We were Barbie Doll friends growing up. In the winter we went down to the duck pond to go ice-skating. We always would see who was the fastest on skates. Afterward we walked home and drank hot coca together. Great times!

I made several more friends in high school, which I thought was great. Then my parents realized it was time for their little Pati to get braces. Braces! Are you kidding me, this would be another source of ridicule. In my junior year, I fell in love. I felt different. Every time he walked by I was so nervous. One time I almost threw up. Oh, that is just lovely!

There was a Sadie Hawkins Dance that year, where the girls asked the boys for a date. I was so nervous. My friends told me to go for it. So one day with nerves in tow, I walked into Donnie's homeroom, with my friends standing outside in the hallway listening. They knew I was going to ask him to the dance. I made it look like I just walked into the room just to say "Hi." He was sitting by the window, reading one of his books. So I started pulling the window shade, and then all of a sudden it just took off, right out of my hand. I could hear giggling from my friends. So with fear and trembling in my voice, I asked him if he would go to the dance with me. To my surprise, he said yes. As I ran out of the room, I kept saying to myself "He said yes, he said yes, he said yes" and then I said, "I will see you later." That's when I felt that little girl just pop out and say, "See I am still here, I just look a little different." As the night of the dance grew closer, I felt I belonged to someone. Was this the Prince Charming that I dreamed about as a little girl?

The night of the dance came and it was cold and gloomy, but to me the sun was shining. The dance was held in November. Donnie and I walked with his best friend and one of my friends to the dance. The walk to the school gym was short, but I felt so wonderful that night. I said to myself, could it get any better than this? Oh yes it could. We had a great night together.

The rest of the year was wonderful and the New Year just got better. The smell of spring in the air, birds singing. My relationship with Donnie took another step. We got very close, nothing like I ever felt before. I used to dream of my Prince Charming on his white horse and I just knew he was finally here.

My junior year was the best ever. I had lots of friends, a guy that loved me and I loved him. He did not care if I had braces, skinny legs and skinny body. He liked me for me, the girl with the very long brown hair and big brown eyes. We went everywhere together.

My friend Pam was nuts about a guy that my boyfriend knew. We would go out on double dates. We girls would dream of us all getting married, living on the same street and our kids playing together. We went to the Junior Prom and stayed out until two in the morning. My parents bought me the prettiest gown I ever saw and Mom took me to her hairdresser. I think she was more excited than I was.

Before Donnie picked me up, I stood in my bedroom, in front of my mirror and just twirled around. I felt like the fairy princesses that my mom read to me about when I was little, but then I stopped, walked up to the mirror and really looked at myself. I saw the little girl was gone. I was looking at a woman. I confess that I cried a bit, but then I rocketed back to the present, feeling so loved and happy. I guess I knew that if I kept crying my makeup would start to run. I finally had a normal life!

Weeks after the prom, my girlfriend Sue and I tried out for the Baton Squad again. We both tried out in our sophomore year and did not make it. That brought a sense of failure, but we talked about it and kept practicing. So after tryouts the following year, we found out through a friend of ours, that we both made it. Laurie said she was not supposed to tell us and we would have to act surprised. They always posted stuff like this on the bulletin boards, in front of the cafeteria. When we found our names on the list, we both started to cry, and hugged everyone that walked by. We had three nights a week in the summer break to learn our routines. I remember getting my boots and getting to those practices. I practiced that baton every waking moment. I walked around the house—broke a few lamps—then my mom moved me to the outside. I walked up and down my street and marched in my backyard. And boy did it pay off!

Some nights my boyfriend, Donnie, would take me to practice, because he had practice with the baseball team. After practice we sat in his car and talked. I just love to talk, talk, talk…. Anyway we talked about our future together. I knew we were entering our senior year in few months, so I wanted to get serious. But he was moving in another direction, a direction called college. I just brushed it aside.

We would go for rides in Donnie's car and he would often bring his brother, Teddy, who had multiple sclerosis. This was the first time I was ever near someone with MS. It was kind of scary for me at first, I was not sure what to expect. I remember seeing him in church and how Donnie would always take such good care of him. I could see he loved his brother very much.

One time my boyfriend came over to pick me up and he had his brother with him. We were going to Danbury to get some 8-track tapes. His brother always sat in the middle of the front seat, so Donnie could take care of him. I sat in the passenger front seat and his brother just smiled at me. I could sense that he wanted to tell me something, but he could not get the words out. So with a lot of love and encouragement from Donnie, he got the words out very slowly and with a lot of effort. He told me that he loved me! My heart felt like it stood still and my eyes filled up with tears. Teddy was just beaming with smiles and love for me. This 12-year-old boy touched my heart. I felt that this precious 12-year-old would never have a relationship like I had with his brother. And yet those words meant so much to me, that almost 44 years later I still remember it fondly. Oh, of course when he told me he loved me, I told him that I loved him too!

September was upon us and so was our senior year in high school. I felt great, looked great, had a great guy and was a member of the Baton Squad. I knew it was going to be the best year of my life! Football season started, my friends were with me—Laurie on the Cheerleading Squad, Sue and I on the Baton Squad. Wow! I loved the sound of the drums starting up before the band. That was our cue to start marching and march we did.

As the football season resumed the feeling of autumn surrounded me. The trees started to turn into God's glorious shades of color. I loved high school, my boyfriend, my friends and my life.

It is said that all good things must end. So did football season. The winter winds blowing off the New England coast brought cold, snow and ice, but it also brought a lot of decisions. Many of my friends were getting ready for college. Yep, even my loving boyfriend! Oh no way! He talked to me about college and what he wanted to do with his life. I said "Wait, what about our life together? Did we not have something here? Didn't you tell me that you loved me? Aren't you supposed to meet someone, fall in love, and get married? Isn't that the way it is supposed to happen?"

That year Christmas for me was not really good, as I feared what was to come down the road. I felt disconnected with Donnie. We still went out and did things together, but I felt, and soon realized, that he was pulling away from me. My heart was breaking into little pieces.

As the weather started to change, so did my life. One of the prettiest times in New England, Spring, was popping all around me. Trees that looked dead were suddenly rich with buds ready to burst open with God's color and love. The flowers popped their tiny little faces from the ground. The birds had new songs to sing. Donnie came over to see me every Saturday afternoon. I used to love listening to the birds on my back porch and watching the sky, just I like when I was a little girl. Oh those white puffy clouds, always so beautiful.

That fateful afternoon I was sitting on my front porch waiting for Donnie to come see me. I was thinking about our phone call a few minutes earlier. He said he needed to talk with me about something important and I had no clue what it was.

He rolled up in his car, got out, hands in his pockets. As he approached me, he pulled his hands out of his pockets and gave me a big hug. I was excited to see him, but something in my heart did not seem right. He sat down and told me he had to break up with me, because in the fall, he would be going away to college. He said it would be too hard to have a long distance relationship and he just could not do that to himself or me. I felt layers of pain enter my heart. He had taken the very thing in my life that was so great and precious to me and was throwing it all away. I could not stop crying.

I hugged him and pleaded with him to give it a chance— and to give me a chance with this college thing. He held me for a few minutes, took both of my arms and looked at me and said, "Pati, I don't think this will work for us. The year I had with you was the best year of my life."

I said, "I thought I was your life?"

Then he said the most hurtful words in the world, "We can still be friends."

Really!! Friends!! How could someone love you so much, then in a few words, it is over? We had a deep relationship and he just wanted to be friends! How does this happen?

Was this a cruel trick that God was pulling on me? I kept asking God how could He let this wonderful guy into my life and then take him away. "What am I going to do now?" These words ran through my mind like waves on an ocean at high tide.

After he kissed me and gave me a hug, I could see tears in his eyes so I knew he was hurting. But not like me. I watched him go to his car and then he stopped to look at me. Then he said good-bye. I was standing on my front porch when my mom came out. I guess she saw what happened. She sat down with me on the porch, put her arm around me and she said, "Pati there are more fish in the sea and someone else will come around."

With tears streaming down my face I told her, "I wanted that fish." I really don't remember the rest of the day. I heard it was one of the prettiest days that year—the Spring of 1971.

My good friend Pam and I shared a locker. When I saw her on Monday morning I told her what happened. We both stood there crying. She said she could not believe what happened and asked me if it was more than just college. I told her that's what he told me.

As the final months of high school approached we still had things to do in school. I tried to avoid the places we would go to together. I knew where his classes were and where he would be after school. But one time I could not help going by his locker. What did I see? He was with another girl! I knew who she was and she knew who I was. How could he do this to me? My heart sunk. He told me that he did not want any relationships because of college and now this. I was crushed! I saw them in the halls together more and more. And then I started to get mad!

One day I saw them together in the hallway and I could not take it anymore. I wanted to hurt him so badly, so I ran up behind him and kicked him the pants! It almost knocked him down. I asked him, "How could you do this to me?" He just walked away.

Later the same day I was at my locker and this girl he was with stopped to talk with me. She told me that she was not serious with him and they only went out as friends. I stopped putting my books away and turned and glared at her. Then I got other books I needed, locked my locker, and blew her off. As I was walking away, I mumbled to myself and thought it was a good thing I didn't say anything. I would have said something cruel to her. What I really wanted to do was haul off and smack her!

For months the senior class was getting ready to put on a school play. Most of my friends were in the play and they told me to try out. I told them, "No way are you going to get my butt on that stage!"

But one day after school was out, there was just a sprinkle of students in the hallways. I saw a friend at the end of a long hallway, and figured school was out, so I screamed her name to get her attention. Well, I did get her attention, but I also got the attention of one of the teachers as well. It was one of the music teachers. She poked her head from around the corner and I knew I was in big trouble. She proceeded to tell me that there was no screaming in the hallways and "Oh, by the way, did you try out for the schools play, little Missy?"

I was kind of taken back with what she said and I just looked at her with a huge question on my face and said, "No way!"

Then she said to me, "Well, honey, I think you just tried out. I need someone who could scream loud and I just found her."

I told her, "No way am I going to be in the stupid play."

So she proceeded to inform me that, "It is either this stupid play or you will be doing detention for a few weeks." Needless to say, I chose wisely, I was her screamer for the play!

Helping out with the play helped me a little bit to forget the pain I was feeling about Donnie, but each day there was still the task of trying to forget. Walking home each day was hard for me. As I walked past the duck pond, I thought of all the times we sat there and talked about our lives together. I used to be excited about the future, but now I really did not know what the future held for me. You know, even the ducks sounded a little different.

I realized that Donnie was not my Prince Charming, so who was? I thought I knew, but I guess not. My heart had been so wounded, I didn't know if I wanted to go there again. I even said God, "Who is he and why is it so important to find him? After all, I have my whole life in front of me—or do I?"

The year 1971 was a very interesting year for me, after Donnie told me our relationship was over, I lost myself in my friends—one in particular. Lucy was another friend I grew up with and she lived about four houses away from mine. I really did not hang out with her too much when I was little, but in high school and getting out of school was a different story.

I was at Lucy's house and we were sitting and talking about the kids in school. But this day was going to be different, because this is the day I was introduced to drugs. Lucy said, "I've been smoking pot for a little while now, and you should try some, Pati." She told me it was very cool, but the biggest thing she said was it made you forget your problems and it feels like nothing can touch you.

When she said that, I answered, "Bingo! That sounds good to me, let's do it!" I told her that was what I had been looking for. Maybe this was my Prince Charming for a while. This would never hurt me, and would never run off to college and leave me. She showed me where she kept it, in a small radio. She took off the back of the radio and that is where she kept her stash. We had some really fun times. One time we went walking in the snow together, walked around an apple farm smoking pot, chasing her dog, with the snowflakes touching our face. What a great night we had!

During the year, there was another guy I became interested in. I had no real thoughts of a permanent relationship, just wanted to have fun with no strings attached. A month or so later, we were having our Senior Prom and some friends of mine asked if I could help with the decorations. I told them I would love to. I was on scaffolding when I heard a voice from below, "Hey Pati, are your going to the prom?"

I knew that voice. He was a good friend of mine, he was such a positive guy, always smiling, laughing and everybody loved him. He had some wild looking hair, too.

He screamed at me again and I told him, "No, I am not going, just helping out today."

"Do you want to go with me—just as friends?"

I said, "Yeah I'll go."

He said, "That is just far out and too groovy."

Another good friend of mine, Boswick, told me I needed to go to the prom and have a good time. He said he was tired of looking at me so upset all the time. From the first day in homeroom class, I was the girl with big smile and funny laugh. Boswick said, "You don't laugh anymore, Pati."

He was one of about 8 black kids in our school. My senior class was around 150, I believe. We had some racial problems, but not huge ones. I really never paid too much attention to racial issues. My parents raised us to respect everyone, no matter what. My friends were excited that I was going to the prom and going to have fun again. I had a great time, but someone I really cared for was not there. I kept thinking why I could not let him go. What was that stronghold? Pati, old girl, I thought, you have been dumped, now just move on. But I still felt like I lost my best friend. I guess I did.

As the Senior Class of 1971 came to a close, the last days at Milford High School were different. The halls looked empty. The hustle and bustle of students was not there anymore. I walked by my ex-boyfriend's locker and a flood of memories hit me. It felt like it was just yesterday that I stood there at his locker waiting for him to get his books and walk me to my class. Just before graduation day the seniors signed yearbooks. A lot of people wanted to sign my yearbook. I thought that was weird, because they never gave me a second look. They signed mine and I signed theirs. One of my friends was not there. She had gotten pregnant. Before she quit school, a lot of people looked down on her, but not me. I was her friend and I was sad that she was not there.

But the shocker of the day was Donnie wanted to sign my yearbook. I wondered what he was going to write. I really don't remember what I wrote in his yearbook. I saw the page he wrote, but could not read it then. I took back my book and gave him his. We just stood there looking at each other for a few seconds, so I took a deep breath, I hugged him liked I never hugged him before and kissed him on the cheek, knowing that this would be the last time I saw him. I cried and told him how much I loved him and to have a good life. He told me the same thing, so as I turned and walked away from him, I left the gym, I looked back one more time to see his face. He smiled and waved goodbye, he too, knowing that this was the last time I would see him. I could see tears in his eyes and that was the day I let him go.

We all have first loves in our lives, and I would never forget this moment. I felt like time was standing still. I remember that long walk back to my locker. As I opened my yearbook to see what he wrote, I slumped to the floor and with tears streaming down my face. I took a deep breath and read, "My dearest Pati, you and I have been through a lot in our junior year and the start of our senior year. The year with you was the greatest in my life. We did so much together and you were the biggest part of my life and I want you to know I did not mean to hurt you, but I needed to move on to college. You were the first girl I really loved and my truest love, and the only other girl I will love next will be my wife. I will always have a special place in my heart for you, which no one can fill. I pray that we can still be friends. Pati, I love you, I guess I always will, but I need to move on. Again, remember this—I love you! Love, Donnie".

I could only sit there and cry. My tears were so strong and heart was breaking all over again. I remember asking God, "Why does this hurt so much? Is this my life now?" I was not going to college like most of my friends. I had no idea what God had in store for my life. I closed my yearbook and just sat on the floor crying.

A few minutes later, Pam came by and sat on the floor with me. "Why are you crying, Pati?" I told her what Donnie just wrote in my yearbook. I told her to read it and she did, then she started to cry. So here we were, two friends sitting side-by-side, on the floor and crying. After a few minutes, we looked at each other and started laughing. We had to do something. So we cleaned out our locker.

We laughed at all the stuff we had crammed into that locker, stuff we had not seen in months. My baton stuff, some books, pictures, and then Pam's stuff. We put it on the floor and started to laugh at how we got all that junk in there. It was very funny. We made a few trips to the garbage. We looked at each other. Both of us heaved a big sigh and closed our locker. We walked by where the football trophies were encased. There was even a football from the early 1900s and a few varsity sweaters. We walked past the Guidance Counselor offices, where they tried to advise me on my journey after high school. But that did not work!

Then Pam and I walked down the beautiful stairs made out of marble and stone and with a push of the doors we left Milford High School for the last time as students. I saw the beautiful duck pond across from the school and felt free.

After graduation, that summer was different. No Donnie, no school, no baton, even some friends were gone. I wondered what I was going to do with my life. We had a graduation party that night. I got caught up with a lot of drugs and drinking. Some of my classmates were talking about what school they got accepted into and what they wanted to do with their lives. The more I heard them talking, the more I drank.

Some of them asked me what college I was going to. Then a person that I did not get along with in high school said, "Oh she is not going to college, she is just a loser."

I started to say something back to her, but someone grabbed me and walked me away from her. He knew I was going to hit her and I said, "Just let me hit her just once, I will never see her again." He moved me faster away from her, because I was kind of fighting with him to let me go, but the more I tried to get away from him, the faster we walked away from that girl. I just wanted to knock her lights out!! Later on I thanked him for saving me from myself.

II

FROM NEW HAVEN TO MR. BLUE EYES

During the summer my parents informed me that if I was not going to college I'd have to start looking for a job. I had no clue where to go. As I sat in my bedroom with my grandmother's old bed and her dresser I looked out my window. I leaned on the windowsill, looked at my backyard and heard all the birds singing their songs for the day. I always loved clothes and thought maybe it would be fun to work at a clothing store. I had a part-time job at a local department store when I was in high school and hoped to get it back. But no luck.

So my first job out of school was working behind the counter at Howard Johnson's. When some of the kids I graduated with—that I did not get along with—came into Howard Johnson's, they asked where I was going. I told them I was not going to college. Some of them made fun of me and made rude comments. They dropped stuff to make me pick it up, and called me a loser. They said, "You were a loser in high school and you will always be a loser, Pati." I couldn't understand why they had to be so mean. So this was what the real world looked like! Why didn't I have the drive to go to college and better myself?

After work I spent my time at Woodmont Beach where the hippies and druggies hung out. I worked days and got high nights. I thought—shaking my head in disgust—this is a nice goal I have for myself. I met Lynn, a girl at work who was looking for a roommate. She lived near the beach. I told my parents I was moving out and Mom cried. My parents told me if I changed my mind, I could always come home. I felt like I could never do anything right, but I knew my parents loved me. So with a few clothes and some stuffed animals, I left that little house along the seashore. As I drove away from the house I grew up in, I realized that I was now a "grown up."

Lynn and I got along pretty well, but she had a situation that I didn't realize. She was going out with a married man. Lynn was 19 and I was, too. I asked how she could go out with a married man. She told me she loved him, and he loved her and was going to leave his wife and family for her.

Okay, I was a little naive, but I was not that stupid! This chick was living in Crazy Land. One night when I came home to change clothes, Lynn's boyfriend was on the phone. I walked right by him. I just wanted to change my clothes and get out of there. I changed into dry clothes and headed out. Suddenly I felt a hand grab me from behind. He threw me on the floor, yelling and screaming at me. "You little whore! You were listening to my phone call, and now I am going to beat the tar out of you!"

"I did not hear your phone call," I screamed. He took my head in his hands and slammed it down on the floor. He pulled about five inches of hair out of my head. Then he smacked me in the face a few times and punched me in the stomach. I tried to run away, but he grabbed my arms and legs. I sobbed, "Stop, please stop! I didn't hear anything!"

He kept pounding me. I punched back and tried to bite him, which made it worse for me. I decided then and there that if I was going to die, I was going down hitting and punching. I was covered with blood. As I tried to crawl to the door he pulled me up, threw me against the wall and grabbed me by the throat. "If you tell anyone what you heard, I'll come and find you—and you know what I'll do!"

I got out the door and he took off in his car. I found a stone wall, sat on it and cried. Steve, a friend of mine, was walking up from the beach. He saw my broken body covered in blood. I was shaking, crying and wiping the blood from my face and eyes. "Pati, what happened to you?" I couldn't stop crying. "We need to get you to the hospital," he said as he helped me off the wall.

I held onto him and pleaded, "No, please, he'll kill me if I do."

Steve looked at me. "What kind of people do you live with?" I asked him to take me to my friend Paul's house, right on the beach. We walked to the beach. When Paul saw me he couldn't believe it. They cleaned me up and put me in a spare bedroom. I didn't return home that night.

That bedroom it was in an old house with lots of windows. My bed was next to one window. The room had a set of beautiful French doors that opened onto a patio. I could hear the waves along the beach and a ship's horn out on Long Island Sound. I could hear the faint sounds of seagulls crying in the night. I felt so alone, so alone. As I lay there thinking about my life and what just happened, I wondered where that little girl was who had so many dreams.

I heard music coming from a house down the street. It made me think of my parents' house. They played music all the time. Then I rolled over, hugged a pillow and cried myself to sleep.

The next day I was supposed to meet with my mom and grandmother and I asked them to meet me at my apartment. When I woke up the next morning my friends made me eat breakfast. I thanked them for taking such good care of me. I walked back to my apartment, hoping Lynn's boyfriend was not going to be there. I just sat on the stone wall in front of my apartment and waited for my mom and grandmother. When Mom stopped the car and saw me they were horrified. "Pati, what happened to you, Sweetie?" I lied and told them that I was in a car and the door was not closed. I fell out of the car. My mom wanted to take me to the hospital, but I refused, telling her I was fine and feeling much better. I didn't want to bring them into this problem or getting hurt either.

I decided to move back home—it was much safer there. A few months later I found a new job in a little clothing boutique in downtown New Haven across from the New

Haven Green and Yale University. The owners were a married couple and extremely nice. She wore her hair up like a huge beehive and was very pretty. We called her "Mrs. Z" and her husband, "Mr. Z." They had parakeets and a dog in the shop. We called the dog "Z-man."

Laurie, my good friend from high school, called and wanted to get together. I told her I could meet for lunch. I was excited to see Laurie—I had so much to tell her. When we met she asked if I wanted to get an apartment with her. I was ready to move out of my parents' house. I knew there was not going to be problems with her, like I had with Lynn.

During our lunch breaks, we sat at the New Haven Green and looked in the paper for rentals. Sometimes we went to the Copper K. It was a Mom and Pop place— a very cool place to go. One day Laurie found an apartment. She called the woman and we went to meet with her. She was a Yale law student going to Europe with her family. She said she would be back the end of the summer, to go back to school. So it was only a rent for four months. I think she liked us. "If you would like to rent it, it's yours," she said. Laurie and I looked at each other and said "yes!" at the same time.

I was doing something positive with my life—a job and an apartment. That summer was very interesting living with Laurie. At night we drank and smoked pot—and some different drugs here and there. But the biggest thing was the pot and drinking. Laurie and I could always be found at a place called Hungry Charlie's. It was right across from Yale University. We got some drugs from the rich kids at Yale, but other times from our friends at Hungry's. There was a cemetery down the street where we would go to smoke pot and listen to the ghost stories about the people that were buried in the cemetery. I knew they were only stories, but some nights Laurie and I were scared to walk back to our apartment!

July 20, 1972 was a day I will never forget, because it changed my life forever. I worked ten hours that day because someone at work called in sick and I was asked to work a few hours more. I didn't mind. I would be getting out at eight o'clock. I got home that night around 8:30. I was very tired and wanted to shower and go to bed. But Laurie wanted to go out and she wouldn't go without me. We had some words and she won. I was just going so she would stop bothering me. We walked to Hungry's that night. Laurie smiled, "Pati, we are going to have a great time, you'll see." There was a guy in front of the bar kissing girls' stomachs. Laurie giggled, "Check this guy out. He is really cute, and boy does he have a nice body!"

When we got near him, he said, "No one gets by me without me kissing your tummy."

Laurie said, "Okay."

Then he turned to me "Okay Little Lady, it's your turn."

"If you touch me, I will knock you out!" I said. I guess I was a challenge. "Hit the road," I continued with a few colorful nicknames. "Laurie," I turned away from him, "I'll meet you in the bar."

When I got into the bar I asked the bartender Ben, "Who is the jerk out front?" He indicated the jerk and I said, "Yes, that guy."

"Oh that is just Geoff. He is harmless. He wouldn't hurt a fly," he smiled.

I said, "Oh so you say!"

Then Laurie came in, "Are you an idiot or something, Pati, what is up with you?" I gave her a disgusted look and lost myself in my drink and the music. Geoff was at the bar talking with Laurie and Ben. Laurie was all over him. I rolled my eyes and had another drink.

A few weeks later Laurie and I went to Westport, Connecticut to a beach called Sherwood Island. It was a really nice place. This day it was very hot and sunny—and very crowded. We stayed about an hour then looked at each other, "Let's get out of here!"

On the way home we stopped for ice cream. Laurie had her mom's car. It had air conditioning, which a lot of people back then did not have. While we were getting ice cream, we noticed four guys getting ice cream, too. They came over to talk with us and asked if we would like to go swimming. Laurie and I agreed. After swimming for a while, one of the guys asked if we would like to hang out with them. We said that we wanted to go home and change and that we would be back.

So we went back to Laurie's parents' house, dropped off her mom's car and took mine. Off we went to New Haven, changed clothes, grabbed a bottle of wine and some pot, and climbed into my 1967 Mustang fastback. It was a beautiful summer night, and as we drove, Laurie and I talked about how cute a few of the guys were.

Suddenly I told Laurie, "You know that guy we saw at Hungry's a few weeks ago, kissing girls' tummies? I don't know what it is, but I think he is going to be there. This is really starting to trip me out. What's going on?"

She just looked at me, "Pati, you are never going to see that guy again. Never. Just get over it." But the more she said that he wasn't going to be there, the more I had a strange feeling that he was going to be there. Laurie saw the look on my face and kept shaking her head and saying, "No way! No way!"

As we turned onto Oriole Lane, we could see the guys hanging out in front of their house like they said. I pulled my car up, and everything felt like slow motion. My car ended up nose-to-nose with a maroon and white Oldsmobile. Laurie screamed, kept hitting my arm and screaming! There were a lot of choice words coming out of her mouth. I was in stun position! I held onto my steering wheel so tight my fingers started to hurt. My mouth hung open, in pure disbelief. I could not believe it. Sitting on the hood of this car, looking right at us, was the guy Laurie said I would never see again. Laurie would not stop hitting my arm. "Pati, how did you know he was going to be here? How did you know? How did you know?" Something was telling my heart, but what?

After sitting there for a few minutes, we got out of the car. Geoff just stared at us for a minute. He looked as shocked as we were. Then he said, "Well, well, well! Look who it is.—the two little chickadees from New Haven!"

One of the guys asked, "Do you guys know each other?" Laurie admitted we saw him two weeks before in New Haven at Hungry's. He thought that was very weird. We started talking and hanging out and cracking jokes.

After a while Geoff asked if anyone wanted to go for a ride in his car. Laurie piped up. "I would," she said and jumped in the front seat.

Geoff asked Laurie, "Does she want to go?" He was looking at me.

I was insulted. "Excuse me, I am standing right here. Ask me." I rolled my eyes and telegraphed Laurie to help me out. I really didn't want to go for a ride.

Laurie said, "Come on, Pati. What else do we have to do?" I guessed she was right, so I climbed in the back seat behind Geoff. Then this goofball guy with red hair climbed in the back with me. As soon as he got into the car, he started to talk, and would not shut up. I even gave him "that look." It said, "you are an idiot, just leave me alone." He was very annoying. Every now and then, Laurie looked at me and smiled. I squinted my eyes at her. She got my mental message, "I'm going to get you for this!"

Laurie started chatting about her old boyfriend and how he dumped her. She told Geoff she wanted to go by his house to see if he was home. Geoff told her, "If you don't stop talking about your old boyfriend, I'm going to kick you out of the car." She wouldn't stop talking.

I stared out the window and wished I were somewhere else. Every now and then I looked up and saw Geoff looking at me in the rear view mirror. When our eyes met, I quickly turned away. One time I saw how blue his eyes were. Geoff looked at me a couple of times and winked. I quickly looked away. I was thinking—I told Laurie this guy was a jerk a few weeks ago, then on the ride over here, I am telling her that I think he is going to be here. Now here I am, sitting in the back seat of his car, and he was winking at me! I started to panic. What was going on here?! Get me out of this car!!!

At first I thought this was stupid—crazy. Just as I was talking myself out of this situation, the car stopped. We were back on Oriole Lane where the guys were. Geoff and Laurie spoke to each other, then Laurie said, "Pati, come on let's go hang out with these other guys." I knew Laurie didn't like the way Geoff talked to her. But these feelings hit me so fast, I was confused, **u**pset. Where did these feelings come from?

Geoff slowly turned around to me. "Do you want to take a ride with me?"

My first thoughts were—Run Pati, Run! But something inside me said it was okay. "Okay," I said. I got into the front seat of Geoff's car and it started to move. I saw Laurie screaming something, but I didn't hear her. We took off. The ride seemed a little weird, yet somehow comforting.

Geoff told me if Laurie still wanted to be with her boyfriend, she should go talk with him. "That's just Laurie!" I said. We rode past the beaches and into West Haven along the seashore. It was a warm summer night—a perfect night in Connecticut. We were getting close to a hot dog place I went to as a kid. He asked if I wanted to eat. It looked like the old time 50s hamburger hangout, and right on the beach. The smell of hot dogs, fries and hamburgers cooking was great. The aroma of salt water from the ocean and hearing the seagulls cry brought back so many pleasant memories.

We got a couple hot dogs and split a serving of fries. He got a soda and I got chocolate milk. He told me he just spent his last five dollars on me. We talked for a very long time. I started to look at him the same way I did with Donnie. I had just met this guy. Why was my heart being drawn to him?

What did this guy have? How did I know he was going to be at that house today?

As Geoff talked again, time seemed to go in slow motion. I kept asking myself if I should trust him? I kept looking at his big blue eyes, thinking there was something more here than long hair, nice body, blue eyes and his car.

Suddenly Geoff asked, "Isn't that your car?"

"Yep that is my car. I told Laurie she could drive it anytime she wanted." He had a shocked look on his face. "What? She is my friend, I trust her," I continued. He just looked at me like I was crazy.

Then we started to talk about other things. He smiled at me, and before I knew it, I–invited him back to my apartment in New Haven. I remember putting music on, and gave myself to him. My heart started to beat so fast. Was I falling in love or something?

Geoff asked for my phone number. He told me he would call me, but I really didn't believe him. I gave him the number and said, "I hope you do."

When Laurie got home that night with my car, I told her what happened. She walked around the room laughing and saying, "Oh, Little Miss Perfect! You wouldn't let him kiss your tummy, but you did this!"

I shrugged my shoulders, smiled and told her, "I think I fell for him tonight."

Laurie said, "Pati, be careful. Guys like that just use girls."

The next day I went to work, Laurie went to her job and we got home around the same time. I told her I was going to take a shower. I was really tired—and worried. I really fell for this guy, but I didn't want to feel like I did with Donnie. Laurie knew about my relationship with Donnie and was concerned for me. As I showered, Laurie screamed and ran into the bathroom. "Pati, guess who is on the phone?"

I wrapped a towel around myself and jumped out of the shower. Still soaking wet, shampoo in my hair, I ran into the living room and grabbed the phone. "Hello?" When I heard Geoff's voice my heart jumped and I knew I was hooked. This man had stolen my heart. I couldn't contain my feelings for him. Was this one my Prince Charming? Did my Prince Charming come in a maroon and white Oldsmobile?

Geoff said he wanted to see me again. I couldn't believe my ears. Was he really talking to me? Did he make a mistake and was trying to call someone else? Why would he like me?

As the weeks went by Geoff and I were together a lot. We were getting very close to one another. I was happy and I could see he was, too.

One summer night we were at Hungry's when Geoff told me that he had to talk with me. My mind flashed back to my parents' front porch with my old boyfriend. I said, "Oh dear God, not again. I just can't take another rejection."

Geoff said, "Let's walk around the Yale campus. I know a place we can sit and talk." As we walked my heart sank. I didn't want to take that walk. I knew if I didn't go, everything would be okay. As we walked, I took a deep breath and asked Geoff what was wrong. He didn't answer me, so I knew something not good was coming. I prayed. "Oh God, please help me!"

We found some beautiful marble steps. I looked around the campus and wondered if the brick and stone walls could talk, what would they say. The lush, green ivy draped over the old brick buildings and the amazing old trees. This could not be happening. Maybe it was nothing at all.

We sat on the marble steps. He took my hand and looked into my eyes. You know that dead silence you hear? I swear I could hear my heart beating. Geoff took a deep breath. "Pati, I am married."

"Married!! Are you kidding me? Married!!!" Geoff said some other words. I only heard "married." I saw my Prince Charming fading away. After what seemed like an eternity I shook my head again. I could actually hear him talking. He told me he was separated from his wife. My first thought—what I wanted to say, "Sure you are, Buddy. You're not separated! You are lying to me!" As he talked I looked into his eyes. I could see he was telling the truth. Geoff told me he married his high school girlfriend and his marriage was wrong from the beginning.

I could see the pain in his eyes. "Pati, I know you can't understand this, but I have to leave my heart in a box, so no one can touch it anymore." No. No. No, No! I could not understand it, but no words came out. He gave me a kiss, told me goodbye, turned and walked away.

With each tear I felt my heart breaking again, again and again. "This is too much," I prayed, "love is too painful. Lord help me!"

I sat there for what seemed like hours. Then I felt a hand on my shoulder, it was Laurie. "Pati, I have been looking all over for you. Everyone said they saw you and

Geoff going out this way." She stopped and looked around. "Where is Geoff?" She put her arm around me and cried with me. She never asked me, but I knew she knew. "Come on, let's go. Our friends are going to East Haven Beach. You need to come with me." I really didn't want to go, but Laurie wouldn't take "no" for an answer. We walked back to Hungry Charlie's.

I sat on the steps of a 1960 hippie looking, multi-colored school bus with the doors open. The busload of our friends left New Haven and headed down Interstate 91 on that beautiful, warm summer night. We got to the beach house, I did not feel like partying. I took a bottle of wine and a blanket and sat on the beach by myself. I listened to the sound of the ocean waves hitting the beach, the buoys on the breakwater, and ever so often I could hear the faint sound of a ship blowing its horn in the distance. I began to feel calm.

Then some guy from the party came out, said it would be okay—and told me that he would fix it for me. I looked at him and said, "Are you crazy or something? You are going to try to fix it for me? Get out of my face and leave me alone!!" But he decided to take up residence next to me on my blanket. I ignored him. I just tried to focus on the stars and a nice warm summer night. Finally I asked him, "Why do guys do that to girls?" He started to give me an explanation, but I turned him off. I could see he was still talking, but to me nothing was coming out of his mouth. I kept thinking what I was going to do.

About three weeks later I was working in the boutique. I told my bosses what happened, because they noticed I had changed a bit. I was not the "Chatty Cathy" I normally was. Mrs. Z noticed I was not smiling like I used to, and I offered to walk the dog around the Yale Campus—before I really never liked to do it. When I walked the dog, I took a joint with me. I only smoked a little bit. It took me back to the days in high school when my friend Lucy introduced me to my new friend, marijuana. It helped back then. I thought maybe it would help again. I was trying to make myself feel better about my stinking life. But that did not work.

One day about a week later, I was working and talking with co-workers in the back stockroom for about an hour when Mrs. Z came running in out of breath."Pati, he is here!

I looked at her like she was some crazy woman. "Who is here?" I asked.

She grabbed my arm and said, "Look!" I peeked out the door. I gasped. It was Geoff! My boss was so excited I thought she was going to pee herself. Mrs. Z said, "Oh Pati, look at him. He is so handsome! And he has a suit on!" I couldn't move and just stared at him. The next thing I knew, my boss pushed me out the door.

I stumbled a little bit, caught myself, and then walked through the store, very slowly. I guess he heard me. When he saw me, he had the biggest smile on his face. He said, "Hello," took a deep breath and slowly said "Can you have lunch with me? I need to talk with you."

Before I could get my answer out, my boss said, "Oh yes, she can go to lunch now. And take your time, Pati." Then she winked at both of us.

I smiled. "Let me get my purse."

As I went behind the desk, Mrs. Z grabbed my arm and whispered in my ear, "He is the one." I wanted to start crying, but I held it in. I smiled at her and told her I would be back. Mrs. Z said "take all the time you need!"

I told myself I was leaving my heart in the box this time. We walked down Chapel Street and kept looking at each other, not really talking. After a few weird minutes, Geoff said, "I've been miserable for the past few weeks. Everything in my life has been going the wrong way. Today I have to go to court. That's why I'm dressed like this."

I listened, then asked, "Why do you have to go to court?"

He said he got caught with a different birth date on his driver's license than the one on his registration. I was puzzled. "What?" Geoff said he was high the night a New Haven cop pulled him over. He told the cop the truth, and he was going to court for forgery. I didn't know what to think. What I heard was, "I am married." I guessed his telling the cop the truth had to count for something.

So as we talked and had lunch, I fell in love all over again. Was it his blue eyes looking at me? Was he really the one? That night he went home with me. Was I doing the right thing? My heart felt it was right. He was the one. Then I second-guessed myself once again.

The end of the summer came. Laurie and I left the apartment we shared. Laurie went back to her parents' house. Geoff and I got an apartment with some people from Hungry's. I think we had seven or eight people living together. We lived there four months and no one ever paid the rent. We got kicked out and I moved back in with my parents. Geoff helped me move some clothes and my grandmother's chair. As he was moving me back home, Geoff had to stop the car because he was so upset. I looked at this man who had tears streaming down his face. I asked him what was wrong. He told me how much he loved me. We would be about 45 minutes away from each other. It was a big deal for both of us. We didn't like the separation. I didn't want to leave him, but this was what we had to do.

When we did see each other, we talked a lot, took walks around Woodmont Beach, and discussed what we wanted out of life. I was working two jobs, so I was able to get a small apartment in West Haven. The majority of the tenants in the complex were older people. I was the only young girl living there. One of the places I worked was a restaurant where Geoff visited me. He sat in the bar, waited for me and became good friends with the bartender, Jimmy.

Geoff followed me home each night to make sure I got home safely. There was no parking lot, so we had to park on the street. One night he followed me home and we talked for a few minutes. I leaned on one of the parking meters because I was tired of standing all night. Geoff said he had to ask me something. The old guilty doubt snuck into my mind. Did I do something wrong? I hoped not. Geoff smiled and looked into my eyes. "Will you marry ….."

Before he could finish his sentence, I screamed, "Would I? Yes! Yes! Yes! I will marry you!!" Then he took me into his arms and swung me around. We started to kiss. I didn't care who saw us. I was happy!! My Prince Charming was finally here and I was going to start my Forever After with him!

On February 14, 1973, Geoff was legally divorced from his wife of 10 months. I told my parents that Geoff asked me to marry him. They were happy—but not happy he was divorced. I told my parents that his first wife cheated on him, kicked him out and was planning to marry her boyfriend.

I met Geoff's parents and they seemed to like me. Geoff said I was a huge change from his first wife. He told me all she did was complain about everything, which drove his parents crazy. He said I was "a breath of fresh air" to them. So I was pretty happy that they liked me.

I told my mom I wanted to wear her wedding gown and she started to cry. (I think I get my crying from her!) When I tried on the gown, it fit perfectly. The only thing I had to change was what I considered was the 1950 era outdated veil. It was great for her, but I wanted something more current. I moved out of the little apartment in West Haven and stayed at my parents' house until we got married. My parents were very happy that I did this.

The day of the wedding finally arrived. I was getting dressed and looking into the mirror, when I saw something was not right. My tongue was totally black! I screamed at the top of my lungs that I was dying. My father flew down the stairs, got his suspenders stuck on the railing. It snapped off and hit him on the back. As Dad entered the room I cried, "I am dying and I will never see Geoff again!!" Dad looked at me and told me to calm down and listen to him. Then he laughed. "Pati, it is just nerves. That happened to me when I married your mother." My mom entered the room and traded glances with my dad. They smiled at me and told me I would be okay.

October 14, 1973 was a beautiful, warm autumn day. On the way to the church, I told my parents I wanted to stay married forever. I sat in the back seat of my parents' car with my mom. Every time she looked at me, she started to cry. I told her to stop crying, because every time I saw her crying, I started to cry—and it would ruin my makeup. I told her the wedding dress was the most beautiful dress I ever saw and I was very happy to be wearing the dress that she wore.

When I walked down the aisle I saw my Prince Charming standing there waiting for me. I was so excited! I had my family and friends with me—and the man of my dreams. The wedding was beautiful. I felt beautiful. After the reception, Geoff and I went back to our apartment and the following day we headed out for our honeymoon to New Hampshire. Geoff told me, "When your dad was walking you down the aisle, I didn't know how old you were, but I figured if he has a smile on his face, you must be of age!" We both thought that was pretty funny. I was a very happy girl!

We got to New Hampshire and it was so pretty, with so many beautiful colors on the trees. The next morning we awoke to snow and ice on the ground. I told Geoff, "Oh no, we didn't pack coats or sweaters!" Geoff didn't have anti-freeze in his car. So that was our honeymoon. We headed back to Southern New England and to our little apartment, with the used, black vinyl couch that rocked back and forth. We had a little kitchen table and chairs that didn't match. We had a bed and a nightstand, and our clothes. It was better than nothing at all. We were happy.

I worked at a restaurant in February 1974 and Geoff worked at the junkyard. I started to feel sick a lot and decided to go to the doctor. He said, "Let's take a pregnancy test."

"Pregnancy test, really?" I was not expecting that. Back in the 70s they did not have the quick pregnancy tests, like they do now. It usually took three or four days to find out. I remember the day so well. I was very anxious to find out the result. I was on my break at work when I called the doctor. I felt like I couldn't breathe. Then the nurse got on the phone and said, "Mrs. Adams, the rabbit died."

I started to cry, "You killed at rabbit—Why?" The nurse laughed. "No, that is an old wives' tale, Mrs. Adams. You are pregnant."

Pregnant, pregnant, pregnant! I was going to have a baby! I thanked the nurse, hung up the phone, ran to the bathroom and cried, then laughed, then cried. I couldn't wait to tell Geoff, so I called him at work.

But the good news was not good for Geoff. There was dead silence on the phone. I asked if he was happy we were going to have a baby. He said, "Pati, I love you, but I am not ready for a baby now." I was so upset. Not ready? He might as well have kicked me in my stomach. When we got home and talked about it, he could see I was excited and very happy. He told me he would try to be happy, too. He said he was scared to have children. As the months passed, I grew bigger and Geoff started to get excited about being a dad. But he was nervous and so was I. We were worried about how to take care of a baby. So we attended birthing classes. They showed us how to prepare before, during and after.

I went into labor two weeks early. Every time they checked me they told Geoff he had to leave the room. Then after each time, they called him back. The last time they checked me, they told him to go downstairs and get some coffee. They told him it would be a while, and they'd call him if anything changed. He came into the room and gave me a kiss, said he was going to get coffee and would be back.

That year at this time, the World Series was going on. The doctor came in and checked me, then went back to watch the game. When the nurse came in to check, she realized I was ready to have the baby. They called the doctor, wheeled me into the delivery room and I was given pain medication. With a couple of pushes our first son, Geoffrey, Jr. was born. But where was Geoff?

They had forgotten to call him back upstairs. After a few minutes I heard Geoff looking for me. When he found out they had forgotten to call him, he was very angry. When he got to the room where I was, our son was wrapped up and lying on my stomach. I was not holding the baby and he started to roll off my stomach. Geoff caught him before he hit the floor. There was no one in the room with me. If Geoff had not gotten there in time, our first-born son would have hit the floor.

When Geoff caught him, he saw his son for the first time. I could see tears in his eyes. I, too, was teary but still kind of out of it from the medication. That little life that we created—what a bundle of love and joy he was.

A few hours later the families started to show up— my parents, Geoff's parents, my grandmother and my two

17-year-old brothers. When my brothers saw their new little nephew, I heard, "Oh wow! A kid. He is really small."

I rolled my eyes and asked, "Is that all you have to say?" Our parents were so happy, and they got to hold him. My mom, mother-in-law and grandmother cried. I even saw tears in my dad's eyes and my father-in-law's eyes.

I kept telling Denise, Geoff's mom, I was sorry I didn't get her a birthday gift. She told me, "You have given me the best birthday gift that anyone could ever give me. You have given my first grandson on my birthday!"

1975 was a blustery winter. Geoff and I were learning how a baby works. We had some rough patches here and there, and were just trying to figure each other out. I spent many hours on the phone with my Mom and my mother in-law. I had so many questions about how to take care of a baby.

Around Geoff, Jr.'s first birthday, I started to feel sick again and told Geoff I thought I needed to see the doctor. I was pregnant again. I was happy and couldn't wait to tell Geoff we were going to have another baby. But when I told Geoff, he was not happy. He said we really could not afford the baby we had. We were really struggling to pay off the medical bills from his birth.

I cried. "What are we going to do?" Geoff told me to go back and talk with Doctor H. So I made another appointment with him. A few days later, I told the doctor that I was happy, but my husband was concerned that we were already having trouble paying off the medical bills.

Then Doctor H told me these words I will never forget. "Well, Pati, you can just have an abortion." I had never heard the word "abortion." I asked him what it was. He said, "Pati, it's just a blood mass right now. Anyway, in 15 minutes you will be back to normal. You will spend a couple hours at the hospital, then you can go home to live a normal life."

I just sat there. I felt like my heart was breaking. But why? The doctor said I would be okay and back to normal. He saw that I was upset and said, "Don't worry about it. You will be fine. It's just a procedure."

So I went home to tell Geoff. He said, "Okay, let's do this." I called Doctor H to make the arrangements to have the procedure done. We took Geoff Jr. to Geoff's parents' house, so they could watch him. Geoff told his parents I was having bleeding problems. I didn't feel right telling them a lie.

I remember walking into the hospital. I was very nervous and shaking. I kept looking at Geoff for reassurance that we were doing the right thing. When they called my name, I got up, I was trembling—shaking. Geoff got up and gave me a hug and said I would be fine. But the look on his face was telling me something very different.

I was brought into a room that was cold and icky. The nurse was not very nice. She told me to put on a hospital gown and lay down on the table. She left the room. I had no medication for this so-called "procedure." Doctor H came in but never spoke to me. He asked the nurse if she was ready. I trusted him and still he spoke not a word to me. They started the machine— I can say to describe it is that it sounded like a vacuum cleaner. The pain was so intense—pain I had never felt before. I recall the sound of that machine and the breaking of my heart.

But why? Could anybody tell me why? I told him to stop. It hurt so much. But the nurse said they couldn't stop. I couldn't believe the pain. I felt cold. My body was shaking so much the nurse had to hold me down. I felt sick to my stomach. I felt dirty—a sense of loss. I couldn't figure out what was happening to me.

Then I heard Doctor H say, "Did I get it all?"

The nurse said, "You are all done." She told me that she would be right back, then she and the doctor walked out of the room, leaving me alone with my legs still in the stirrups. I heard the sound of the machine winding down. I couldn't stop crying, I just lay there, looking at the ceiling. I wanted to crawl into one of the tiny holes in the ceiling and die. My heart felt like someone had ripped it out of me. I was still shaking and crying.

When the machine finally stopped its noise, I looked around to see it. I had to use the hospital gown to wipe my face and my eyes, so I could see a jar with a tube in it. I saw there was something in it. But what was it? I thought it might be the blood mass the doctor told me about. After what seemed like an eternity, the nurse returned. I asked her what was in the jar. She told me, "Just be quiet. It's nothing at all."

They wheeled me into a recovery room, where I laid on my side and cried into my pillow and sheets. I was cramping and felt sick to my stomach. They gave me crackers and ginger ale. That seemed to work a little. Then they told me I could go home. Geoff was waiting for me in the waiting room. When I looked at him, I saw he had a great sadness in his eyes. I saw him very differently then. I kept looking at him, thinking, he was supposed to help me, take care of me, be my knight in shining armor. Where were you?

As we drove home, nothing was said. I stared out the window and noticed my reflection looked a little different. I was not the happy young girl I used to be. Something was stripped from me, but what was that something? I looked at Geoff a few times and he could not look at me. He drove with his hand on his forehead. We went to pick up Geoff Jr. His parents asked how I was. They came out to the car and could see I had been crying. They both gave me a hug and said I would be okay. I just sat there with a blank look on my face knowing that I just lied to them. I felt like my insides were screaming and no one was listening. Geoff told them I would be okay and just needed to get some rest. So that is how we started the rest of our lives, with a big fat lie! For what?

For the next two weeks I couldn't sleep. I had the same dream two weeks in a row. Every time I closed my eyes it was the same one. I dreamed I was walking along a lovely street filled with overflowing flowerpots. Blossoms were dotted along people's walkways. I heard birds singing so sweetly. The air smelled wonderful. I felt a gentle, warm breeze on my face. My long, brown hair-was flowing ever so gently.

All of a sudden I was standing in front of a cemetery. The birds stopped singing. The flowers were gone. The gentle breeze turned into a cold, biting wind. The sky turned dark and I heard thunder and saw lightning. I looked around and couldn't believe where I was. Something was drawing me into the cemetery and I did not want to go. Something was pushing me into this dark place. The more I said I didn't want to be there, the more something drew me to a tombstone. I brushed away the ivy and leaves from it. Then I fell to my knees crying. I was not prepared to see what I was looking at. Written on the tombstone it said, "ADAMS BABY."

What was I reading and why was I reading this? Is this why I was feeling so terrible? Was this a baby? Why didn't Doctor H. tell me the truth? I thought doctors had to tell their patients the truth. He was supposed to help me. Didn't he take an oath to help and save people's lives? I woke up screaming and in a cold sweat every night. I didn't want to go back to sleep. I didn't want to go back to that cemetery.

After two weeks of nightmares, they stopped as fast as they showed up. My life with Geoff was crazy. We were still hanging out with friends that did drugs and drank. We hit the bars every now and then. Geoff Jr. got shipped to Grandma's house each time. When Geoff Jr. started to walk, I had no patience to deal with him. I tried the best I could.

Summer of 1976 arrived and I was pregnant again. Geoff and I talked and decided to keep this child. The day I went into labor, I was at my mother-in- law's house. I was talking with her and her neighbor. Geoff was cleaning out his car and Geoff Jr. was taking a nap. I kept asking what time–it was. Fifteen minutes later I would ask again and finally Denise asked, "Are you timing contractions?" I told her I thought so.

I called the doctor and was told, "Come right away."

I went back out to talk with the ladies. They asked what the doctor said. I told them, "Oh, the office said to come in."

Denise and the neighbor asked, "Did you tell Geoff yet?"

I said, "Oh, no I will wait until he finishes cleaning the car."

My mother-in-law Denise told Geoff and he said, "What? Are you crazy? Let's get going!" He threw stuff into the garage, washed his hands and told me to get into the car. When we got to the doctor's office they took me in right away. After they examined me, the doctor told Geoff to take me across the street to the hospital. He said I was in labor and I needed to get to the hospital immediately.

I asked if I had time to go home and wash my hair. He said, "Pati, you can, if you want to have that baby in the shower." I suddenly realized his baby was coming fast. Geoff took me to the hospital, parked the car and came up to my room. The doctor and nurse told him to wait outside.

Geoff said, "The last time we were here you told me to do the same thing. I am not leaving the room. Do what you need to do. I am staying here. I am not going to miss this baby's birth!" Once they realized that he wasn't going to leave, they did what they had to do. Within a few minutes, the nurse came in, called another nurse and said they needed to get me into the delivery room immediately!

Geoff put on a hospital gown, hat and mask and came in with me. The doctor showed up just in time, and with a few pushes, our son Michael was born. I was crying. Geoff was crying. And so was little Michael. The nurse put Michael in a bassinet. He was crying, so Geoff leaned over to him and said, "Hello Baby. How are you? Hello! Michael." He immediately stopped crying. We had another precious little son!

The nurse turned around and said, "What did you say to him? I've never seen anything like that before."

Geoff said, "I have been leaning on my wife's tummy and talking to him every day, so he remembers my voice." He said he wanted to do that with our first son, but never got the chance.

My parents, grandma and Geoff's parents came to see him. My grandmother smiled at me. "Now you have given me two great-grandsons. Is the next one going to be my great-granddaughter? I hope so."

Tony and Robert could not be there that time. They were both in the Navy.

III

SMOKE AND MIRRORS

Well, our lives only changed a little. Every other weekend both kids were shipped off to Grandma's so we could party some more. Geoff and I worked on our marriage. I thought, well, this is my life—I am going to try to enjoy it. We did things with the kids, took them for rides in the car and to the beach. They played with other little kids—just did kid stuff.

But something was happening with me and I couldn't figure it out. Then it happened. I was pregnant again—so in a crisis again. We had another abortion.

And a year later, pregnant again. Another abortion. You are probably wondering why after all the pain I went through with my first abortion, why would I have two more. During this time of my life, I was at a point of no longer caring what I did and why I did it. I guess you could say I was just numb and mindless having these two more abortions. I know it does not make any sense. But at this point in my life, nothing I did made any sense any more. I had no self-esteem, no self worth. I felt I was living in this deep, dark, black hole with no way out. I could not wrap my mind around the fact that these were my babies. To be very honest, the more Doctor H. told me it was just a blood mass, the easier it was to just keep believing him!

But the last two abortions were different. I had a lot of medical problems. I had to return to the hospital both times because I was bleeding and it would not stop. Doctor H, on both occasions, had left parts of the pregnancy. I was told they did not get everything the first time, so I had to endure it all over again.

The nightmares returned, night after night. In these nightmares, before I got to the cemetery I was weeping. When I got there, I fell to my knees and brushed away the leaves covering the tombstone. It read, "ADAMS BABIES." I realized at each of those moments, that those were babies—my babies—my children—and not just a "blood mass" like Doctor H told me. How could I have done this again? Why didn't someone help me? Didn't anybody care?

I started to close my life to others—my husband and my kids. Geoff and I fought all the time. Our relationship started to go downhill. I couldn't figure out what was happening to our marriage. My wonderful life was slipping away and my Prince Charming fell off his horse. How did we end up like this?

We fought into the 80s. I told Geoff I had to go to Florida and get away for a while, to find myself again. Geoff hung in there, hoping I would come back a new person. I did come back a new person, but that person was temporary.

Three times I took off on him and three times I came back thinking I was okay. Finally the day came. "Geoff, I have had enough. I want a divorce."

Before I left to find myself, Geoff was racing cars—drag racing. I was attracted to one of his friends, because he was paying attention to me. I knew I would find someone to love again—but his friend?

Geoff and I were separated and I got up every morning at 4:30 to be at the babysitter's house by 5:30, because I had to be at work at 6:00. I really hadn't gotten too far with my life. I worked at the same restaurant where I worked after I graduated high school. I guess I didn't go very far. I remembered some of my "friends" calling me a loser. I did feel like a loser. Life was very tough for me at this point.

I traded the old Cadillac we both loved for a new red Ford Mustang. It felt good. I was accomplishing something on my own. Geoff took the boys every other weekend to his mom and dad's house where he lived. I tried to fight the feelings I still had for Geoff. I knew it would soon pass. He fell off that white shining steed and never got back on.

Geoff would leave the boys at his parents' house and go to a bar. It was called the Office Café, but the Milford Police Department nicknamed it the "Bucket of Blood." They often found people dead in the parking lot or in the bathrooms. Geoff bought a Harley Davidson and started to ride with old friends.

The week before Thanksgiving of 1978, when Geoff brought the boys home, I asked if would he stay for a minute and told him I had to ask him a question. We put the boys to bed and sat on the couch. "Geoff, I really miss you and I still love you. Would you please take me back?"

He looked at me quietly for a few minutes. I wondered why he was taking so long to answer. I expected a simple, "Yes, I will." But Geoff said, "No, I can't do that. You've hurt me for the last time. I can't take it anymore, I've moved on with my life and you should too, Pati." I couldn't breathe. I felt like I just got sucker-punched. Then he said, "I've got to go. I'll see you later." He walked away and left me standing there at the door of the apartment we used to share. Numb, I walked into the boys' room, looked at my two sweet babies sleeping, leaned over and gave them each a goodnight kiss.

I walked out of their room, closed the door and in the hallway I slumped to the floor and wept bitterly. My heart felt like someone had ripped it out of my body. I kept pounding the floor, saying, "Dear God No! No! No! What happened to my marriage? What happened to us? Why did I make the biggest mistake of my life? What about our boys, what am I going to do now? I have lost him forever. Help me, please God, help me! I cannot lose Geoff! Make this pain stop!! I kept wiping the tears flowing down my face, but the more I wiped, they faster the tears came. I got up and staggered around the apartment, still weeping. Everywhere I looked were memories of Geoff, our boys and me together. My heart was broken again and my life was shattered.

That Christmas Eve of 1978, Geoff brought the boys home as he did every other weekend. This time he asked if he could come in and talk. "Okay," I said, "but just for a few minutes."

Geoff told me to put the boys to bed and said he'd wait in the living room. When I returned he was sitting on one end of the couch. I sat on the other end. For a few minutes he didn't say anything. I thought—oh, this is going great. If this goes on a few more minutes I will get up and walk into the other room. Then he said, "Pati, I have been missing you so much. I want to try to work this out with you. I still love you!"

I couldn't get to the other side of couch fast enough. I wrapped my arms around him and kept hugging him. I could not believe what I heard. I was longing to hear those words for so long. I felt alive again. My life seemed to matter again. Before I felt rejected and now I felt wanted! And my boys—our boys. Thank God we could be a family again! Did God hear my plea? Did God see my tears? I could not stop crying. The hole that I felt in my heart was filled up with, "Pati, I have been missing you so much and I still love you!!"

I was so happy! I cried and told him I loved him so much, too! I told him how very sorry I was for doing this to him and our two sons. Geoff stayed the night. And the next morning I felt alive, happy and loved! It was the love we had before we were married—and the love I felt for him the day we were married. When Geoff Jr. and Michael got up, they were happy to see Mommy and Daddy together again.

This happened a week before our divorce was final. The separation lasted four very long months.

Yes, life can get crazier. The bar that Geoff went to when he dropped the boys at his mom's house was the first place he introduced me to his new world. I was uneasy about how everyone would treat me, but with Geoff by my side, nothing could hurt me. He introduced me to his biker buddies. They kept calling him "Crazy" or "Craze."

"Why do they call you 'Crazy?'" I asked.

"The first time I was here I took the money off the pool table. People had put it there as they waited their turn to play. I wiped off the names on the blackboard, and in big letters I wrote 'CRAZY.' So from that point that's what they called me."

I thought these people were pretty cool and very down to earth. Geoff went to the bar to get us drinks. I saw a girl put her arm around him. He immediately stopped her and motioned me to join him. He turned to the girl and said, "I want you to meet someone." He put his arm around my waist. "This is my wife, Pati."

I learned that a few weeks earlier Geoff told her he was still in love with his wife. My first reaction was to rip her hair out and smack her in the face. Then I remembered that I was the "dumper." I never touched her. I was nice, but I did give her looks up one side and down the other.

This was the start of our new life together. A lot of our biker friends had kids our kids' age, so that was pretty cool. We had really good Memorial Days at Sandi and John's place. Loud music played, beer flowed, the smell of pot in the air—and the kids.

The kids always tried to sneak beer. It was not easy for them because our biker friends knew that the kids could not drink. The kids— being kids—figured if anybody asked what they were doing they'd just say they were getting beer for Mom or Dad. Yeah, Right!! When people got wise to them, they would yell for Geoff, me, Sandi or John.

Sandi and I sounded so much alike it would really freak the kids out. It was pretty funny. Sometimes they looked like little bugs running for cover! For amusement they reverted to watermelon fights, hanging out near all the Harleys or going down to the beach. So Geoff, Jr., Michael, Eric, Johnny, Jennifer and Melissa waited for the point in time when their parents got non-functional, and when they knew that they could get away with anything.

But there was a good friend of ours named Rodney. We called him "Bones." He got the nickname because he had so many motorcycle accidents he had broken almost every bone in his body. He never called us, the parents—he just got on the kids' case, right there. When the kids saw Rodney they knew the jig was up.

When Geoff and I were separated, Sandi had a huge part in getting Geoff and me back together. There were a lot of times when Geoff was in the bar, that John and Sandi were there. He spent many hours telling Sandi how much he still loved me, but just could not go back with me, because of the pain I caused him. Sandi encouraged Geoff to go back with me and work this out. She told him that we were still a family, with two little boys that need care from both of us. She could see how much he still loved me. When I found out what she had done, I told her, "There is no way that I could ever repay you for the encouragement and help you gave to Geoff." From that point on we became best friends.

Saturday night was our official night out. We barhopped with our biker friends, usually spending an hour or so at each bar. One night Jerry, the owner of the Office Café asked Geoff and me if we would like to work at the bar on Friday and Saturday nights—Geoff as a bouncer and me as a bartender. Jerry knew that, with Geoff as one of the bouncers, there would not be any trouble in the bar. Geoff is 6'2", with lots of muscle and he wouldn't take any garbage from anyone. The boys spent weekends at their grandparents' house. I drove them over in my car. Geoff followed me on his bike. I'd leave my car and take off on the bike.

One night was a little crazier than usual. People were yelling and playing pool. Music was loud, smoke filled the bar and there was a smell of pot. I spoke with customers and did shots with friends. Jerry knew we would be drinking, but told us to keep it to a minimum. I never took him seriously. On that night I was drinking and smoking pot a little more than usual. There was a kitchen on my side of the bar. I called Geoff and we snuck in there to smoke. Some friends brought cocaine in, which was what I preferred.

I was pretty lit up and had a big attitude for being 5'4". I felt six feet tall that night. Geoff was throwing out a guy who was starting a fight. Jerry told the bouncers, "If there are any fights—out they go."

That night there seemed to be more fights than usual. About 1:00 a.m. the owner decided to lock the cash register the bartenders were using.. He went downstairs to his office. I saw this and, as he descended the stairs I yelled, "Hey, how are we supposed to make change for the customers?"

"You and Donna can use your tip money for change."

I just stood there and said, "I don't think so, Buddy!" My temper flared and I screamed obscenities as he disappeared into his office. I screamed, "Get your butt back up here, Jerry." He ignored me! It was "last call" for alcohol and the bar was packed. Harleys started up outside and Geoff was busy throwing more guys out the door.

I was about to come unglued and wanted to do something, so I grabbed a brand new gallon bottle of whiskey. People saw I was upset. They cheered me on. Then it happened. I hummed that bottle across the back of the bar, where all the liquor bottles were and where there was a 20-foot mirror backsplash. It cracked into a whole bunch of pieces. I just stood there smiling, with my arms crossed. I thought I was some kind of little toughie. "I'll fix his butt," I cursed. I felt pretty darn good about myself.

I heard people screaming, "Yeah, Pati!!!" Clapping, whooping and hollering. This got Jerry's attention and he came running up the stairs.

Geoff was in the middle of throwing someone out the door and heard the crash of the bottle. He saw me jumping up and down, screaming obscenities, my long hair flying around, looking like a crazy woman. "Pati, what the hell did you do?"

Jerry was in shock. Customers were yelling, "Jerry, what are you going to do now, you wimp?" He told Geoff he was calling the cops.

Geoff tried to hold me back from punching Jerry. I squirmed and screamed insults. "Go ahead and call the cops," I told him. "They should arrest you for being an idiot!" Obscenities flew out of my mouth and I couldn't stop. Jerry did call the cops.

Geoff got my purse and we headed out the door. The cops showed up with three cop cars. "What is the problem here?" one huge officer asked.

Jerry pointed to me. "It's her, I want her arrested!" I screamed, swore and hollered like some kind of lunatic.

The cop walked me to the police car, put me in the back seat and was about to put handcuffs on me. He turned around to Jerry. "What do you want me to do here?"

Geoff and the bar manager pleaded with Jerry not to press charges, but I kept swearing at Jerry. Geoff had enough and stuck his head in the police car. I'd never seen that look on his face. He told me if I didn't shut my mouth I was going to jail. I started to cry.

Twenty minutes later the cops got sick and tired of all the shouting back and forth. "Look Pal," they said to Jerry, "what do you want us to do with her?"

I sat in the back seat with tears streaming down my face. "I am so sorry."

Finally Jerry said, "If you guys pay me back for the damages done, I won't press charges."

Geoff said, "Yes, we'll both will pay for the damages, won't we, Pati?" I nodded.

Everyone was looking at me, especially the police officers. "Do you agree with this arrangement and understand it?"

I cried and nodded my head. "Yes." The officer helped me out of the car. Jerry told us we could work it off in the bar. He was going to use our hourly pay for the mirror but he said I could keep my tips. We agreed to a payment of $600.00. This was said in front of the police officers.

Geoff went back to get my leather jacket that I forgot while I waited with the bikes and some friends. He came out with my leathers and started up the bike. There were five or six Harleys warming up before we took off. It was about 2:30 in the morning so we decided to go out for breakfast. Geoff shook his head. "Let's go. Get on." As we rode off, Geoff asked, "What in the world happened to you tonight? I've never seen you like that. You turned into a wild woman".

"I was ticked off," I answered. "Let's leave it at that!!"

"You'd better not do this again!" Geoff said. I promised not to break any more mirrors. But no one was going to tell me what to do! The last time I listened to Geoff my world fell apart. I was going to do what I wanted. Then I thanked Geoff for getting me out of a real tough spot.

We rode down some winding roads. I closed my eyes, listened to the night, smelled the gas from the bikes, heard the thunder-like roar of other Harleys with no mufflers, and felt the crisp night air on my face. My hands were in my leather jacket pockets. I could feel the biting wind and took a deep breath.

What was I doing with my life? I wanted to wipe my face because it started to get wet. I thought it was dew from the night air. There were tears streaming down my face. I wanted to brush them away, but it was too cold. So they stayed on my face as a reminder of what I was feeling at that moment. How did my life get so out of control? What was I thinking? How was I treating my husband? How was I treating my boys? What kind of wife and mother was I?

Seven months later we realized we needed a clean break from the biker and bar scene. The bars were nothing but drama and a whole lot of trouble. A local bike club wanted to recruit Geoff and said they would take care of him and his family. But he did not want to put a target on his back. When they couldn't get to him, they came to me. We never joined them. We decided this was the kind of drama we didn't need in our lives. We finished paying Jerry for the mirror and told some friends at the bar we wouldn't be coming back. It was getting way too out of control.

A year later we decided to move away from West Haven and were able to build a house in Clinton. We were finally getting everything together. We sold our house in West Haven and moved in with Geoff's folks for a few months. In September we moved into a motel in Clinton, because we needed to get the boys registered for school. The builder took more time than he said he would. We expected to be in the two-bedroom motel for a month, but the house was still not ready by October. We had to move into an efficiency apartment for another two months. We got on each other's nerves.

Finally on December 18th, we moved into our new home. I loved it and life started to make sense. Geoff and I were getting along. The boys were making friends. Both boys were on baseball teams and they seemed to be having a great time. All we needed was a white picket fence. But Geoff and I got so wrapped up in our own lives, we forgot about the kids' lives.

Geoff Jr. started to get in trouble with some of his friends. He took Michael with him sometimes. Other times he'd leave his brother alone in the house, which he was not supposed to do. Geoff worked for a local railroad with hours from four to midnight. He left the house at 3:00 p.m. I worked days and came home around 6:00 p.m. So the boys were alone for a few hours each day.

When we got to Clinton, the boys joined the local baseball teams. Geoff was Assistant Coach for a while. Some days Geoff Jr. and Michael each wanted me to attend their games. Occasionally their games were at the same time—in different locations. I had to split my time during the games. I hated to do this, but couldn't think of anything else to do. I wanted to be there for both of my boys. We tried to be normal parents and hated to leave them home alone after school. I thought they couldn't get in too much trouble at home. We soon found out the error of our belief. Geoff Jr's grades were going down, his friends were older and wilder. Michael acted a little differently. Something was going on with our boys.

One time Geoff Jr. was in the kitchen acting funny. I saw him standing in front of the refrigerator door, staring. I knew what was happening because I did the same thing after I smoked pot. We confronted him and he denied the whole thing.

Geoff said, "Boy, don't lie to me!" One thing Geoff didn't tolerate was the boys lying to him. The fighting between them two got worse and more frequent. We couldn't figure out what was wrong with our sons.

IV

SO YOU WANT TO BE A ROCK STAR ?

Our lives seemed to go on with no direction. There had to be more to life. Get married, have kids, live in the same house, then die of old age. When we lived in West Haven, I became friends with Libby, a lady one house down from mine. Libby and I went to hear her son Kevin play, and his band was pretty good. I got caught up in the music. My life, again, was about to change. When I was a child, my mother taped me as I sang and played the guitar. I was not very good, but my mother thought I was. I told Libby I always wanted to do something like this. She told me to go talk to Kevin. The doubts kicked in—how stupid is this? What am I thinking? I'm a grown woman, married with two kids, had I lost my mind?

I made the call and told Kevin what I wanted to do. I asked if he could write me a few songs and he agreed. I hung up the phone and looked out my kitchen window.

What was I doing? But I actually felt good about it. When I told Geoff, he was very upset. I remembered the night on that Harley—no one was ever going to tell me what to do again!

Kevin called and said he laid down some tracks and to come listen to them. What I heard was really good. I asked how did we get this thing going. Kevin said if we wanted to go somewhere with this music, we needed money. I could see things coming together. I had to talk to my husband. I was a little nervous about telling Geoff, but I told him this could change our lives for the better. We could buy a bigger sailboat, put the boys through college and have no more money problems. He saw how excited I was and agreed to take a second mortgage on our house. I got my money.

We decided to use a professional recording studio. I did some of my own backup vocals, and Kevin found more backup vocalists. During the months of recording, my sons came into the studio a few times. Mom was going to be a Rock Star! When we finally got to hear the whole thing put together, it sounded so great I cried. It was a dream about to come true. Geoff heard it and said it was good. Geoff Jr. and Michael were beside themselves. It was on vinyl and it was a record!

As the weeks progressed, problems escalated in the Adams household. I couldn't understand why Geoff wasn't happy for me. Everyone else was—even our sons! But the person I wanted most in this world to be for me—with me, and just plain on my side, was not with me at all.

I also worked at a local restaurant during this time. They nicknamed me "Morticia" from the <u>Addams Family</u>

show. Joe, one of the cooks, sometimes got a little testy. On one occasion as I walked into the kitchen I heard, "Duck! Morticia!" I knew that meant, "Squat down and just keep walking." A bowl of pasta sailed across the room. He was not mean. Joe was really a nice guy—that was just him. Many times Joe and Sam, the other cook, would bang on the server table in the kitchen to get a waitress' attention. Many times, while taking a customer's order, I would hear them banging on the table, screaming, "Morticia, your order is up!" My customers would ask who they were screaming for, adding it sounded like they were saying "Morticia." I'd laugh a little and told them they were calling me, because my last name was Adams.

Joe and Sam were like a comedy team in the kitchen. Sam would make a rude comment and they would burst out laughing. Sometimes they couldn't stop laughing. Then of course, the waitresses commented. One waitress, Judy, was so uncomfortable that she used the pay phone to call in her orders!

A few months later, I started to feel very tired and run down. I felt a lump in my breast. My first thoughts were, oh dear God, I hope I don't have cancer!

I made an appointment to see my doctor. The day of the appointment I was a bit nervous, but as I explained to my doctor what was going on, he said, "I don't think this is serious, but let me examine you." After he examined me, he said, "Everything seems to look okay, but I want run some tests on you." He said he was going to do some x-rays, blood work and maybe do a biopsy later, if need be. He looked confident that nothing was seriously wrong, but I still was nervous. I knew there was a lump! His words, "Seems to look okay," resounded in my mind. I was not comforted by those words. I left the doctor's office, half in a fog.

The house was empty. The boys were in school and Geoff was at work, so I just sat on the couch looking out the picture window at the beautiful trees, plants and little shrubs that God made. As I stared out the window, curled up in fetal position, I felt like a dark cloud was approaching quickly. What was the point of living? What was the point of all this music stuff? Geoff wasn't happy and my marriage was suffering again! I was leaving my kids home alone way too much. There I sat waiting to hear from my doctor! I was always struggling to just maintain, and now just maintaining was not good enough. Now a possible medical problem on top of all of this? I felt like I was slipping further into this dark hole, with no way out and spiraling out of control. All of a sudden I didn't care anymore. I didn't care who loved me anymore. I didn't care who my friends were anymore. Why should I care for people, family and stuff? Why? It was just not worth it anymore! I didn't feel good enough for anyone to love—even me.

I felt so alone, like Geoff was abandoning me. Now my health might be abandoning me. I cried out to God, "Where are You, I thought You loved me, I was told You loved me when I was a child. Did my parents lie to me? How could You do this to me? Have You now abandoned me, too?" I felt so alone, so abandoned and all I did was cry. My heart was breaking in a million pieces.

Now I had to wait. But for what?

Was I going to learn I had cancer and only months to live? I knew others that found lumps. They were okay. But others whose doctors found cancer had given them only months to live. Doctor H. never mentioned the words "cancer" or "dying," but in my mind, that was no other alternative. The stuff that was rolling around in my mind was scary to handle. Was I reading too much into this?

Should I pretend that everything is okay or do I sit around and wait? As I pondered this issue, I realized I needed to move on. Sitting around the house feeling sorry for myself was not me! I chose to tell myself that everything was going to be okay.

So I decided to move forward with the music stuff. I drove to West Haven and my musician friends were working on more songs. Something nagged at me and I couldn't put my finger on it. My voice sounded terrible. My heart was not in it. I decided to take time off and do some more thinking. I drove home in tears. I thought I was getting so close to my dream— and I felt it slipping right through my fingers.

In the next weeks I tried to figure out what was going on with me about this possible music career. And I still did not hear from the doctor's office. The silence was deafening. I walked around the house, wondering if I should pick up the phone and call the doctor's office. I helped the boys with their homework only to find out the next day, that what I helped them with was wrong. I got dates wrong for the boys' appointments. I'd get to work at the restaurant and screw up my customers' orders. I blew through a couple of red lights, not paying attention to my driving. What was the point and what the heck was I doing?

During the time I waited, one day as I sat on our back porch I recalled special days of my childhood—the day I met Geoff, our wedding day, the days our sons Geoff Jr. and Michael were born—and then the nightmare days of my three abortions. As I sat there I leaned my head back on the pillows and saw the same white puffy clouds I saw as a kid.

As they floated lazily by, I could feel my heart breaking once again. I was alone with no purpose for my life. I searched my mind for ways to end my life. We had pills, but I didn't think I could swallow all of them. I saw the carving knives in my kitchen, but the thought of how messy it would be and, God help me, I wouldn't want my boys to find me like that! I could drive my car into a bridge abutment, but I may take innocent people with me. The more I thought about ending my life, the more my heart kept telling me I had many reasons to keep my life.

One day during the long period of waiting for the results of the tests, I walked into the bathroom and just stood there, looking into the mirror. It seemed that for the very first time I saw myself. I had a great dream as a little girl. Now I almost had it in my hand. I thought about Geoff, Geoff Jr. and Michael. What was going on with me? Was I ready to lose my family for a dream that may not happen? Regardless of my future health issues, I had to make a decision.

Just then, my two boys came home from school. I heard them open the back door, run upstairs, scream, "Mom, we're home! We are getting a snack." I heard them in the kitchen getting their snacks, then I heard the back door slam shut. As I looked out the bathroom window, I saw them in the back yard playing with their friends. They were having a great time. Then it hit me! Was I really willing to give them up? I closed my eyes and recalled the day they were born—and the look on Geoff's face when he held them in his arms. At this point the answer became very easily. There was no way I could give up my family for music.

When I made the decision to give up my dream, I felt my life take a turn in the right direction. I knew my life with my family meant more to me than any dream. The late hours and so much time away from home finally reached the boiling point. Geoff talked about moving to Florida-and told me I was welcome to come with him. "Either way, Pati, I am taking the boys out of this madness," he informed me one day.

When Geoff came home that night, I told him I had to talk with him. I saw the look on his face—oh no not again! I told him that my so-called "music career" was over and I didn't want to lose him or the boys chasing a dream that may or may not come true. Geoff broke down and cried. We hugged for a very long time—something we had not done lately. We called the boys into the living room and told them the news. They were a little upset that about my decision, but I think they were secretly longing to have their mom back.

The day I met with Kevin to tell him of my decision was the day my doctor called. Doctor H. told me all the tests were negative. Interesting too, the lump I had disappeared. After days of anticipation, during which I made a choice, which again changed the direction of my life, I was relieved and thanked God for good news.

I drove past the shore and it seemed that I got a little extra dose of courage. When I walked into the studio room, I took a deep breath and told the group I had made a big decision. "My family has to come first," I said. "I've had some serious thinking time, and I'm sorry, but I have to give up the music." We talked for a few more minutes and said our goodbye. I got into my car, sat there and then I closed my eyes, but I knew I was doing the right thing. I thought of the days my parents took me to Savin Rock to ride on the Flying Horses, with the wind in my hair and reaching for the brass ring. As the ride slowed with the brass ring in sight, I could see my mom and dad waving at me with huge smiles on their faces, arms out to me. I opened my eyes. I was not going for the brass ring anymore.

About a month later, Geoff said we needed a vacation. We took the boys to Disney World in Orlando, Florida. I saw Cinderella's Castle. Oddly, it made me sad and happy at the same time. "Why are you crying, Mom?" the boys laughed at me. It was no use telling them about my mom reading books to me about Cinderella and Prince Charming.

Geoff's parents were with us, which made the vacation even better. After a week at Disney World, Geoff's parents took the boys back to New England. Geoff and I took a much needed trip by ourselves to Ft. Myers and Sanibel Island. Just being there alone with Geoff, walking on the white sandy beaches, picking up seashells—and we fell in love all over again. We toured Sanibel Island and had some wonderful seafood dinners. One night we sat on the beach and witnessed an unbelievable thunderstorm rolling over the Gulf of Mexico.

I was really starting to like the south. Geoff did too. He was born in Texas, raised in Southern California. We talked a little about moving to Florida and getting jobs.

Back in Connecticut Geoff, who was on day shift at this time, changed to working nights. He went to air-conditioning school during the day. We put the beautiful home that we had built, up for sale. Geoff finished air-conditioning school. Within a few months we had an offer on the house. Before we moved out of our house, Geoff and I went back to Florida alone. We gave ourselves three days to find jobs and a house. And we did!

We had teary goodbyes with family and friends. One of my best friends, Libby, came to say goodbye and she had her daughter Ally with her. Ally had grown up with Geoff Jr. and Michael. She would come over to our house to see if the "guys" were home. Geoff Jr. was around six, Michael around four, and Ally was around three. Every now and then when I heard banging on the front door I'd check it out and see no one there. A few minutes later, the banging would resume. The door was half screen and half solid door. I was looking out the screen. When I opened the door there was little Ally, with a big smile asking, "Is the guys home?" The three of them were best buddies. The sad part of moving is leaving family and good friends behind.

It was a very long trip, but we made it to Florida and when the boys saw the house with a great big swimming pool, they adjusted pretty quickly. I knew this was a new start for all of us and I hoped we made the right move.

A few months later something ugly crept back into the Adams household. Geoff Jr. got into some pretty crazy things. The way he dressed, his long hair, black ripped t-shirts, spandex shorts and wearing a paper clip as a pierced earring made us uncomfortable. His yelling, screaming at us, playing music louder when asked to turn it down, skipping high school, stealing for drugs became his way of life. This is what we dealt with before we moved, and again in Florida he was attracted the same type of friends. The only thing different was the geography.

Michael was making friends. For the most part, they seemed to be okay. Michael got onto a baseball team, but I knew he was missing his friends back home. He tried out for a football team. He had never played football, but he was tall and big for his age. The coach told him what to do, but really never took the time to teach him. Michael was in with older, experienced kids. So after a few injuries, he quit.

We were trying to get our lives back on track. Geoff and I both worked days. We provided the boys with house keys. They were supposed to get into the house after school, get snacks and do their homework. When Geoff and I came home from work we planned to eat together as a family. Simple, right?

Well, all hell broke loose in our house. Geoff Jr. brought kids into the house, neglected his homework and just acted irresponsibly. I came home from work and found seven to ten kids in the house, the refrigerator open, food missing and loud music playing, kids swimming in the pool and Geoff Jr. nowhere to be found. Other times when he was home, he yelled and hit his brother. It was too much.

Every morning Geoff took Geoff Jr. to school and walked him into his homeroom to make sure he got in school. As soon as Geoff walked out of the front door, Geoff Jr. walked out the back door. Our son was getting into trouble left and right. Lee County Sheriff's deputies came to our house many times. I was, unhappily, on a first name basis with some the officers.

Michael walked to school. He never gave us any trouble. However, the yelling and screaming between brothers was getting out of hand. Michael fought back. I could see that he had enough. Stuff was tossed across the room—Geoff Jr. hitting Michael as he held his electric guitar. When his dad saw this, he grabbed Geoff Jr. and threw him across the room. After that incident, Geoff had to walk away, afraid that, when he was angry he might kill his son. Another time I came home and found a giant snake in my pool. I thought I would lose my mind.

Geoff Jr. had a habit of running away. He would be gone anywhere from just a few days to weeks at a time. His name was on the Nationwide Runaway List three times. When he was home, some days we locked him out of the house. Earrings, bracelets, and brooches turned up missing.

I was afraid to be in the house alone with Geoff Jr. I really thought he was going to kill me and I even tried to keep Michael away from him. One day I just had enough— my last button was pushed—I was done with the craziness. I took all of Geoff Jr.'s clothing and threw them out on the front lawn, screaming uncontrollably through the tears, "Geoffrey, you can never come back to this house again and I really don't care what happens to you anymore. You are tearing this family apart. I wish to God that I never had you!!"

He screamed back at me. "I wish I'd never been born! I hate you both and my stupid brother, too!" He took off down the street in tears, carrying some of his stuff.

As I stood there watching him go down the street I wondered what was happening to my family. I looked around at the beautiful blue sky and the palm trees blowing in the warm breeze and I knew nothing had changed— only the scenery once again.

A couple weeks later, there was a knock at the door. It was Geoff Jr.'s girlfriend, Becky. Between sobs she gasped, "The car in is the house. The car in is the house!" I motioned to her to come in, and told her to calm down. Sobbing, she repeated, "The car in is the house!" I was very upset because she made no sense. I was about to usher her out the door when she screamed. "Wait, they really drove a car into Al's house!!"

I was stopped in my tracks. I grabbed my purse. "Where?" Together we ran off the front porch toward the driveway. "Get in my car!" I yelled.

I couldn't believe what I saw when I pulled up to Al's house. Smoke billowed from the windows—and a car was literally in the house!

When I got out of my car, I could see the car in the back of the house. I walked through what used to be a garage and saw the back end of the car in the kitchen. I moved wires away and stepped into water—probably should not have done that—and rubble of broken walls and broken glass. Through the kitchen I saw the car and where the refrigerator and stove had been pushed into the living room.

I stood there for an eternity. The longer I stayed at the house, the angrier I got. When Al's mother came home, she started to cry and pick up her stuff as she walked through the rubble. She picked up pillows, broken picture frames, broken dishes. Then she asked, "What happened to my son, Al? Is he okay?" I told her Al and Geoff Jr. were not anywhere to be found. They just took off. I had no idea if either of them were hurt.

I told Al's mother I was going to get my husband. We didn't know what to do. Someone had called the Fire Department. When I got home Geoff was just getting home from work. I told him what happened. He couldn't believe what I was saying to him. He immediately started to yell, walk around the driveway, and scream at Geoff Jr. as if he was there. Then he got into the car and drove to the Al's house.

We both hoped that Geoff Jr. was not driving. At this point, I really was not concerned about him being injured! I just had enough!! We were thinking the owner of the rental house could sue us for the damages. Al and Geoff Jr. were nowhere to be found.

Geoff and I got to the house. "Oh no! Oh no!" The Sheriff and the Fire Department were already there. They told us there was no threat of fire because they had cut the power to the house.

When Michael learned of the situation, he closed his eyes and shook his head. "No way had my brother done this!" But he admitted he had not seen his brother in days.

We later learned that Al's mom told the boys not to use the car, because the brakes didn't work. Al and Geoff Jr decided to take the car out anyway for a joy ride and decided to use the emergency brake each time they had to stop. The Sheriff's office told us they had to be going 30 miles per hour when the car hit the garage. And the reason they could not stop was because the emergency brake quit working. Geoff Jr. was not driving the car.

I cried myself to sleep that night. Geoff was so angry, he couldn't sleep. The next day we called the Sheriff's Department to talk about the situation. When the police officer showed up at our house, I asked if there was anything we could do about Geoff, Jr. The officer told us we could place him as a ward of the state of Florida, basically divorcing our own son. We agreed. "Yes, let's do this." We were at the end of our rope. The officer told us we might look into a place called Outreach. He explained it was where kids go that are into drugs, drinking and bad behavior. He said they might be able to help.

The next day we called and made an appointment. Two days later, as we drove onto the driveway at Outreach, I felt like I was going to be sick. What had I done wrong? I got out of the car and the warm breeze hit my face. All I wanted to do was run—just run as fast as I could. As we entered the building, a young man approached us. We told him we had an appointment to see Dr. Kenny. He took our names. I kept thinking it's November, what if he headed up north? What was he wearing? What I am doing, thinking of this? He could be dead for all I know! Dear God help me!

A few minutes later a woman came up to us and introduced herself as Cheryl. We walked into her office. I felt like I was going to be sick, my stomach felt like it had a huge hole—a pit. Cheryl asked us what was going on with our son. We told her, and she explained the program to us.

> My mind drifted away. I remembered when Geoff Jr. and Michael were little guys and the fun we had with them. I recalled when the boys took their first steps, their first words. When they climbed onto our bed asking, "Are you up yet?" The hugs and their tiny hands cupping my face saying, "I love you, Mommy." How proud they were of their first snowman, playing catch with Dad—ferry rides to Block Island and Long Island.

My mind jumped back to the present. Now here we sat. How did we get here? I did not hear a word that Cheryl was saying. I was glad Geoff listened. He leaned over and took my hand. All I could do was cry. Cheryl said what we were considering was best for the whole family. She explained the program helped the whole family, not just the child. She told us the cost of the program. Geoff and I looked at each other and shook our heads. Cheryl explained that Geoff Jr. would not be going home at first. He had to earn the right to go home again. We met Dr. Kenny. He said they would be there for us if we made the decision to put Geoff Jr. in the program.

We got in the car. Neither of us said a word. We were both numb. I looked out the window and cried. Geoff drove with his arm out the window and his hand on his forehead. A few times I looked at him and I could see tears rolling down his face. "Pati, how did we get here?" he asked softly.

Funny I thought, I was just thinking the same thing. As we drove and tried to digest what we just heard, our son was still missing. We had no idea if he was dead or alive. "Geoff, maybe this is a waste of time. For all we know he could be dead. He has never been missing this long." I looked out the window and wiped the tears from my cheeks.

We went to Geoff's parents' house to tell them what was going on, and to pick up Michael. I could see in Michael's face he was upset and very concerned about his brother. We told Geoff's parents about the program and how much it would cost to get this help. Then I called my parents who lived in Port St. Lucie, on the east coast of Florida. I told them how the meeting went and what it would cost.

Our parents decided to help out. So with the money in hand, we went back to Outreach, gave them the money, and told them we still had to find Geoff Jr. They did say if we ended up not using their services, the money would be returned.

About a week later, the phone rang at two o'clock in the morning. I picked up the receiver, "This is the Orlando Police Department calling. Do you have a son named Geoffrey Adams, Jr.?" When I heard his name I felt like I was falling off a cliff. My heart was beating so fast I could not catch my breath. Geoff saw the look on my face and took the phone.

"Yes." Pause.

"Yes." Pause.

"Yes." Pause

"Yes— okay." Pause.

"Yes —okay."

I had no clue if Geoff Jr. was dead or alive. Then I heard, "Okay, how long can he stay there before we have to pick him up?"

Pick him up? Is he dead? "Oh, God please no," I prayed. Geoff told the officer on the phone that we were looking at a program to help our son. We needed to get in touch with them so we could bring him directly there.

Geoff Jr. was not dead! He was still alive. "Thank you, God!"

But what was going on? Geoff hung up the phone "He is in Orlando and he is alive. The police found him under a railroad bridge sleeping with bums. He is wearing only a pair of shorts and sneakers, no shirt."

That morning Geoff called Outreach to let them know that we found our son. The Outreach staff told us we had until six o'clock that night to bring him to the Center. We called the Orlando Police Department and said we were on our way to pick him up.

We drove Michael to school and arranged for him to stay at a friend's house after school. My stomach did flip-flops as we drove the 158 miles to pick up Geoff Jr. We were ready to get this kid some help. We talked on the way to Orlando about what to say to our son. We couldn't tell him he was not coming home. Outreach was going to be his new home for a long time. We didn't want to lie to him, so we decided to tell him that we were all going to get counseling.

When we got to the Juvenile Hall, we signed some papers and the officer went to get him. For what seemed like eternity we sat there expectantly holding hands. The doors flew open and there was the officer followed by a dirty and smelly boy. He looked like he had never taken a bath in his life. He was wearing shorts, no shirt, sneakers, had long matted hair and smelled really awful. I could hardly see him through my tears. I hugged him and told him how much I loved him. He just kept backing away from me. Geoff hugged him and said, "Let's go."

Usually rides in the car with family were fun, but today was not one of those days. I looked out the window, not knowing what to say. Geoff drove and did the same thing. Geoff Jr. wanted to say something, but then he stopped. With a lot of pain in his voice, he finally asked, "Are we going home?"

Geoff told him "We made an appointment to see a counselor. We want to talk with them about our problem."

"I don't have any problem. You guys are my problem," he yelled. When he realized he was not getting anywhere with us, his tone and speech slowed down. Then he asked if he could get something to eat. He told us he hadn't eaten in a few days. We stopped, but did not let him out of the car, believing he would just take off again. While Geoff went to get something for him to eat, I tried talking to him. I told him we loved him, and thought maybe we all needed help. The more I talked, the more agitated he became. Then he asked me why I was crying so much. I shrugged my shoulders and said nothing.

As we turned into the Center, I took a deep breath and asked God for help. We got out of the car. Geoff Jr. was not wearing his shoes. We told him he needed to put on his sneakers. After a short, unpleasant difference of opinion, finally Geoff Jr. complied with our request.

We sat in the waiting room and in my heart I knew our lives were about to change once again. Cheryl came out with two teenagers, the size of NFL players. They talked with Geoff Jr. for a minute. "Hey, come with us and you'll see your parents in a few minutes."

So off he went, not knowing his life was about to change. Cheryl took Geoff and me to Dr. Kenny's office. He explained what was happening. I could hear Geoff Jr. screaming, swearing and yelling. It sounded like furniture being thrown across a room. I started to shake, cry and feel sick to my stomach.

My mind went back to the day we brought him home from the hospital—cute, tiny and smelling like baby powder. Now I had to trust the well-being of my son to the hands of others. I told Dr. Kenny I wanted to see him. He firmly stated it was really not a good idea. I wouldn't take "no" for an answer. Geoff told me he didn't think it was a good idea either. I said, "No, I want to see our son!" Dr. Kenny warned we might not be prepared on what we saw. He told us to go ahead.

Cheryl knocked on the door. It opened very slowly. I saw furniture all over the place and Geoff Jr. standing in the middle of the room, with tears running down his very dirty face. I cried uncontrollably as I walked up to him to tell how much I loved him and prayed that he would get better. He spit in my face, told me I was a whore and hoped I would just drop dead.

Geoff walked up to him and poked him in the chest, which made him step back a few feet. With a very harsh tone, his dad told him to get better and that he loved him very much and, "You are where you need to be." We left him there in the room. As we got in the car and drove the long road back home, I asked Geoff, "Did we just do the right thing? I feel like we just abandoned him."

On the ride home, my insides screamed, "God, why are You letting this happen to our family? Do You not love us?" Everything was going in slow motion, the sky looked eerie and every now and then I saw a flash of lighting. The night was a slow moving nightmare. A nightmare, of our son being gone—with no hope—that I have just abandoned and left for dead. A nightmare that I could not wake up from.

The next day we shopped with Geoff's parents for some clothes to send to Geoff Jr. Denise was so kind. She told me he needed to be there getting the help they could provide. But I still felt like I abandoned my son.

As the weeks went by the holidays descended upon us. I sank into a depression. When we had family talks, I just sat there. I couldn't cook dinner for the three of us. When I did, all I did was cry. When Michael and Geoff wanted us to watch TV, I wandered off to my bedroom and sat there looking out the window. It was very quiet in our house. Michael was quiet, too.

I felt abandoned and asked God why. No answer. Thanksgiving and Christmas came and went with no Geoff Jr. It was 1990. We saw our son on Friday nights at the Center. This was a Seven-Step program. Every Friday night they would have what is called an "open meeting." Parents, siblings and grandparents sat on one side of the room. The kids in the program sat on the other side.

We met with a counselor before the open meeting. Michael sat with other siblings before the meeting. The staff asked each of us how we were doing. They told us how things went with our son, and listened to what we all wanted to say. Each family stood up as one with a microphone and spoke to their son or daughter, who was not allowed to respond. They could only stand and listen. Sometimes they cried. Sometimes they stood there like they did not want to hear.

When a child was doing well, before parents started to speak, the child would yell, "Second Phase" or "Third Phase" and so on, which indicated progress to the Seventh Step.

As long as the child was in First Phase, he would be away from the family home. With Geoff Jr. we saw no change for months. I thought he was just not trying. But one Friday night everyone was telling us that Geoff Jr. had changed. That Friday night open meeting we did not see him. Suddenly Geoff grabbed me. "Look, there he is. He cut his hair all off!" He had worn his hair past his shoulders!

When it came to our turn to talk with the microphone, Michael, Geoff and I stood up. Geoff and I cried and told him how proud we were of him. Michael did what brothers do. He laughed and said, "Nice hair cut!"

Weeks later we attended another Friday night open meeting. When it was our turn to talk, Geoff, Jr. yelled out, "Second Phase!" That meant he could start coming home at night! Part of the program was that when a child achieved a higher phase, the family became house parents to kids that were still on First Phase. We had become Outreach Parents!

Every day we brought him back to the program. Each night he returned to us with one or two boys. Before we had kids in our home, it was checked out by Outreach. There was no alcohol or drugs in our home. Spoons were the only tableware the boys could use. Wherever Geoff Jr. went in the house, the others had to be with him. No excuses were accepted. They had to be in sight of Geoff Jr. at all times.

One boy was giving Geoff Jr. a lot of trouble. We talked with him. He kept telling us he was going to run away. One night he did. First we called the Lee County Sheriff's Department, and then we called Outreach. There were alarms on our windows and doors, but when a kid wanted to run, alarms would not stop him.

A few weeks later at an open meeting, we found out that Geoff Jr. was put back on First Phase for not following the rules. I was extremely upset. It seemed we were never going to be free of all this stuff in our lives. I was tired of trying. Nothing was working. Still another Friday night and Geoff Jr. was still on First Phase.

Some of the families went to a restaurant for pie and coffee after the open meeting. Geoff, Michael and I went with a few other families and tried to enjoy the rest of the evening. I was talking to a lady named Linda and Geoff was talking with her husband Walt. "You know, Walt, sometimes when we are singing during open meeting, it feels almost like church—sort of cleansing." The next week Walt gave Geoff tapes of their Pastor from church.

Geoff thanked him for the tapes and put them on his dresser where they stayed for a few weeks. Geoff told me about the tapes and suggested we might listen to them.

I laughed. "Yeah, right. Not me, Brother. I really don't care about God. I've been asking Him for help and He is nowhere to be found! I am more concerned about our son than listening to some stupid, dumb tapes."

A few weeks later as I was getting ready for a meeting, I noticed the tapes on Geoff's dresser. As I started to walk out the door, something brought me back into the room. I stopped and stared at the tapes. I grabbed one and off I went to the meeting. I did not listen to the tape. Oh, it was playing, but I was not listening. It was nonsense to me.

After the meeting, the thunderstorm we were having stopped and the streets were nice and dry. The sky was clear. It was a beautiful, starry night in southern Florida. I stopped for gas and noticed the temperature was 82°. I loved those nights in southern Florida.

As I turned the car onto McGregor Boulevard, I was half-listening to the tape. Something grabbed my attention. The words I heard radically changed my life forever. "Jesus says, 'Behold I stand at the door and knock. If anyone hears My voice and opens the door, I will come in to him and dine with him, and he with Me.'"

I started to weep uncontrollably. I pulled the car to the side of the road and cried out to God. "Lord, I want You in my life. I have messed up my whole life and I cannot do this anymore. I am such a sinner. I believe in You. I need You!"

When I heard on the tape "Here I am!" and realized it was Jesus knocking at the door to my heart. I bowed my head and talked to Jesus Christ in my simple way. I told Him I was so sorry for what I did and needed Him in my life. Tears rolled down my cheeks and onto my clothes.

For the first time in my life, this made sense. I felt like a bird that was locked up in a cage my whole life—and suddenly the cage door flew open. I could spread my wings and fly! I felt that chains were taken off of me. My heart had a sense of lightness to it. That was something I never felt before in my life. The date was January 20, 1991 at 9:15 p.m. on McGregor Boulevard in Fort Myers, Florida— about two houses away from Thomas Edison's summer home.

I could not wait to get home and tell Geoff. I hit the driveway on two wheels, ran into our living room waving the tape I just heard. I felt like I was going to burst. Geoff saw my smile and excitement. "What is going on with you?" I told him what happened and he looked at me like I had lost my mind. "Oh you, little Miss, 'I don't want nothing to do with God'—and now this!"

"I'm going to call Linda and tell her what just happened." I knew Geoff was not getting it. But I also knew God had miraculously changed my life in that split second. She was so excited for me she could hardly contain herself. She told me that Walt wanted to talk with Geoff.

Walt asked Geoff if we would like to go to church with them on Sunday. He offered to treat us to breakfast. Geoff agreed. "Free breakfast? We will be there!" So that Sunday morning we were introduced to church. When we got there, Walt and Linda heard that Pastor Holbrook was not going to be at church that day. A visiting pastor was going to preach. Linda and Walt were very disappointed.

Then, unexpectedly Walt saw Pastor Holbrook. "They told us that you were not going to be here this morning," he said as they shook hands.

"I wasn't supposed to be, but the visiting preacher got called back home. So you guys get me today!" Our friends were very happy because they wanted us to hear him preaching, and then meet him after church. We sat in the second pew. I was a little intimidated by the size of the church. There were a lot of people in attendance. When Pastor Holbrook got up to preach he said, "Well, I must confess that I'm not prepared to preach this morning. Our visiting preacher was called back home in the middle of the night. I am just going to pull out one of my old faithful sermons" He was preaching for about five minutes, when I looked over at Geoff and I couldn't believe what I saw. His eyes were filled with tears. He clutched the seat in front of him for dear life. Pastor Holbrook stopped and addressed Geoff. "Son, are you okay?" I signaled the Pastor to keep going.

At the end of the service the Pastor addressed the whole congregation. "Anyone that doesn't know Jesus Christ as their Savior and would like to know more, please come up front." Geoff could not get out of his seat. When the service was over, Walt asked if we would like to meet the Pastor. Geoff nodded his head. When Pastor Holbrook turned around to meet us, all my husband could do was cry. Pastor said, "Would you like to go to a counseling room and I will pray with you?"

Geoff said, "Yes." He told Pastor Holbrook he was sick and tired of being sick and tired. That day—January 26, 1991—my husband trusted Jesus Christ as his Savior! After all the crying was over, we left that church new people—and we had a lot of questions. Pastor Holbrook said he would visit our house during the week to check up on us.

Then we went out and got our free breakfast!

Tuesday rolled around and so did Pastor Holbrook. He told us he was going to check up on us and he did! We had lots of questions about the Bible. He answered them the best he knew. He was a very down-to-earth preacher, with a soft southern accent and it was easy to see that he loved God's word. He had gentleness about him and a true love for Jesus Christ. He told us that he was only a man—and man can lead you astray. He suggested we check it out in the Bible for ourselves. We did. Everything we read in the Bible matched up with what he was telling us. God had just removed my blinders. I could see the beauty in this world that I could not see before.

During our conversation with Pastor Holbrook, Michael was kind of hanging around the hallway, listening. We asked him if he wanted to come and sit with us and talk to Pastor Holbrook. He said no, but I knew he heard most of our conversation.

During the rest of the week, Geoff and I talked for many hours about what happened to us in the past week. I talked to Geoff, not at him and he did the same with me. We were kinder to each other. Michael saw the change in his parents. We asked him if he would like to come to church with us on Sunday. He came with us every Sunday. We had more meals together, conversation was pleasant, and we were not fighting about Geoff Jr. and where he was. It was like a breath of fresh air.

V

MAMA LOVES CATS

I sat back one day, thought about my life, and looked at what I had. I realized a huge change had taken place. I cried about all the stuff I did that was wrong in my life. But my heart felt like it was missing something. I cried for all the good things I'd been given and now I had Jesus Christ! Some weekends we drove over to my parents' house in Port St. Lucie on the east coast of Florida. They had just built a new house on a piece of property they purchased years before. It was everything my mom wanted— things they could never afford before.

I wanted to talk to Mom and Dad about Jesus Christ, but I struggled about how to tell them. My mom heard my heart and I think she got it. We had really nice times at their new house. It felt like home to me.

Geoff Jr. was still in Outreach and we had many kids coming into our house. Even though we had a few more runaways, things seemed to be going good. The best day was when Geoff Jr. made Seventh Phase. Graduation Day arrived on a Friday night during open meeting. Geoff, Michael and I, my parents and Geoff's parents were there. We stood up in front of the families and kids and talked about Geoff Jr. We each told a little story about him to everyone. We presented him with a gold chain with a "7" on it to remind him where he came from and all he had accomplished.

The best parts for me were the meetings on First Phase each Friday night, and meeting other parents whose kids were on the same phase as Geoff Jr. We met with counselors about what happened each week with our son and what we wanted to say to him. Michael went in and talked about how he felt. This helped our family in a huge way. Those first meetings were the nights we started to get our son back, Michael got his brother back and our parents got their grandson back!

In October 1991 things were looking pretty calm in our household. We attended church on Sundays and met new people. One night when I came home from work Geoff told me my dad called. My mom had fallen and was in the hospital—but she was doing okay and not to worry. It was late, so I called Dad the next day. That morning I had a bad feeling about what happened to my mom. When I spoke with my dad he reassured me that she was doing fine and I didn't need to come out.

It was a four-hour drive from Cape Coral to Port St. Lucie. Something just didn't feel right. I called Geoff into the room. "We've got to go!" I called my dad and said that we would be on our way within the hour. When we got to my parents' house, Dad was waiting for us. I stopped at the hospital gift store before we went up to Mom's room. I had to get something—it was her birthday. I saw the perfect gift —a T-shirt with a cat on it, because Momma loves cats! We surprised her. She was really happy to see us. She had a few bruises from falling. The doctor said he needed to run some more tests. If everything looked okay, she would go home on Tuesday.

We had a wonderful visit. Mom loved her cat shirt. I did her nails and brushed her hair while we sat around and talked. I told her she looked good for just turning 70. She smiled. It was getting time to go and Dad was getting very tired. As I leaned over to kiss her goodbye something felt weird. Mom told me how much she loved me. Although I heard it many times before, this time was different. Leaving the room was very difficult, but I knew I couldn't stay. I was the last one to walk out of the room and turned to blow her a kiss. I told her I loved her again and said goodbye. I blew her another kiss and she grabbed it out of the air and held it close. We smiled at each other and I walked away.

We stayed the night at my parents' house, but had to leave early the next morning. I told my dad, "I love you. We'll see you soon," I hugged him. "I'll call when we get home." I called and told him we made it home okay. I was going to call Mom, but it was late and I figured she was, most likely, sleeping.

Monday night I was at a meeting at a friend's house. Around eight o'clock, I realized that I kept looking at my watch, like I was waiting for something. The meeting ran overtime and at 8:45 I called Geoff to tell him I'd be leaving in a few minutes. "Your dad called," he told me. "He sounded very strange on the phone." I asked if Dad was okay. Geoff said, "I don't think so."

I tried to call my dad, but got no answer. I tried a few more times, and still no answer. I knew if he were home he would answer the phone. I decided to call the hospital and talk to Mom, thinking maybe she knew what was going on. My mother's phone in her hospital room rang and rang. I called again with the same result. So I called the nurses' station. A nurse put me on hold. Then I talked to another nurse, who put me on hold. Finally, a third nurse answered the phone and was about to put me on hold again. This time I was furious and screamed, "Do not put me on hold again! I want to talk with my mom! Can you ring her?"

I was put on hold again, and then a man spoke into the phone. "This is Doctor Wyatt."

I yelled, "Look, I just want to talk with my mom! Do you have a problem with this?" There was dead silence.

"Please tell me who is calling," he said quietly

"This is Pati Adams. I want to speak with my mother, and I am not happy about being put on hold every time I ask," I told him.

"Is someone with you, Mrs. Adams?"

"I am not alone. Stop with the 50 million questions and let me talk to my mom." More silence.

"Pati, I do not normally like to do this by phone, but your mother passed away about 20 minutes ago." I could not speak. "Miss Adams, are you there? Are you there?"

I held the arm of my friend and began to weep uncontrollably. I couldn't breathe. I gulped huge mouthfuls of air and fell to the floor. My friend yelled to her husband to pick up the phone.

My friends called Geoff and told him what happened. They asked him to come and get me because they didn't want me to drive home. When Geoff arrived at the house, he wrapped his arms around me and wouldn't let me go. "Honey, let's go home. The boys and my parents are waiting for us." Our friends told us if we needed anything to let them know. Geoff thanked them and we drove home.

I couldn't sit still in the car. I stuck my head out the window then sat still. Then I stuck my head out the window again. "I think I am going to be sick!" I pounded on the dashboard of the car. I yelled, cried and screamed. "Why? Why?"

We arrived home and I walked into the house. The first person to walk up to me was Denise. She hugged me and we cried. My sons stood there and watched me fall apart. They didn't know what to do. I hugged them and told them I loved them. They each told me, with quiet voices, they loved me, too.

After a few minutes, I told everyone I needed to call my dad. He answered the phone, crying. I couldn't understand what he was saying. "Geoff and I will be leaving our house in about an hour to be with you," I said. "Please make sure your doors are locked. I'll call from the convenience store down the road from your house, Dad, I love you." Geoff's parents told us the boys could stay with them until we figured out what we were going to do. We took our friend's car to Port St. Lucie, because my car wouldn't make the four-hour trip. I was having car trouble for the past few months. It seemed to run okay around town, but on the highway or long trips, it messed up. We were grateful for the use of my friend's car.

We threw some clothes in an overnight bag and headed for my Dad's. Geoff drove. A few miles outside of Ft. Myers he said, "Pati, I can't drive, I am starting to fall asleep." He'd been up since 4:30 that morning. I glanced at the dash—it was 1:00 o'clock.

"Just pull the car over and I'll drive."

"Honey, I feel so bad doing this. You shouldn't be driving either."

We got to a spot where we could switch seats. As I walked around to the driver's seat, I looked at the stars. I couldn't believe how bright they were! I wiped tears from my eyes and prayed, "God, I can't drive tonight! I need help." Just before I got into the car, I noticed one star stood out from all the rest. It was twinkling so much I thought I was losing my mind. Calmness fell over me. "My mom is up there with you, Jesus!" Then, "Mom, I love you so much and someday I hope I see you again."

The next thing I remember was pulling up in front of the convenience store to call my dad. When the car stopped, Geoff woke up. "How did we get here so fast?"

"I don't know. I don't remember driving the car. The last thing I remember is standing outside the car and looking at the night sky."

Geoff looked at me in amazement. "Thank you, God, for getting us here safely," he prayed softly.

I called Dad and told him we were at the store and would be there in a few minutes. As we pulled up into the driveway, I wondered how Dad was taking this. "My poor dad. My poor dad," I whispered. We walked into the house. Dad was standing in the middle of the living room. He looked as if he had aged 100 years. I hugged him for a long time. I could feel his body falling apart. Geoff hugged him and I started to cry again. "We'll be here for you, no matter what." I saw how exhausted he was. "You need to get some rest, Dad."

He attempted a weak smile and said, "I just can't believe my Mary is gone!"

Geoff and I told him how much we loved him. It was very early in the morning, and I told Dad to go try to get some sleep. Geoff and I went into the guest bedroom to try to get some sleep too. Geoff held me until I drifted off. I woke up around nine o'clock and heard Dad puttering around in the kitchen. He was crying as he went from one counter to the next. I wondered how he was going to get through all of this and how I would to get through it. I decided that we needed to eat, so I put a pot of coffee on and Geoff prepared eggs and toast.

Dad said we needed to call my brothers. He'd called them earlier, but wanted to talk with them further. After he talked with them, he gave me the phone. We agreed Mom needed to be buried back home in Connecticut. Dad called the hospital to tell them what funeral home to use in Port St. Lucie.

That morning we went to the funeral home to make arrangements. The man we talked with was extremely nice and very soft spoken. He told us what he needed from us. Next we had to select a casket. Dad told the man that Mom wouldn't be buried in Florida, that there were family plots in Connecticut. All of a sudden I was horrified. I felt sick. I couldn't be part of choosing a coffin! Dad saw the look on my face. "Pati, if you want to stay here, Geoff can come with me."

"No Dad, I will stay by your side no matter what." As we approached the rooms where the caskets were, my knees got weak and I was not feeling too well. I knew my dad needed me. It was no time to think about myself. The undertaker explained the different prices and the color choices for outside and inside the casket.

Dad saw a silver one with pink inside. "Pati, what do you think? I think your mom would like this one with pink in it."

"Dad I think so, too." So we chose that one. The funeral director told us we needed to pick out an outfit for my mom. We said goodbye and left for home.

Choosing the outfit was the hardest thing to do. Dad stood in the middle of the closet and put his hands to his face and the tears flowed. "Pati, could you do this for me? Pick something your mother would like." He sat on a chair in their bedroom and I brought outfits out for him to see. "Try another one," he said, over and over again. Finally I saw something I liked, a dress and sweater that Mom wore together. He agreed. "She always liked that dress and sweater together. Let's take that." We booked airline reservations for the whole family and arrange for storage on the plane for the casket.

Two days later Geoff's parents and our boys arrived at my parents' house. The next day we drove to West Palm Beach

Airport. It was a painful experience for the whole family. Mom was a veteran—she served in the Army Air Corps—so the American Flag was to be draped across her coffin.

My grandmother told us she didn't want to come to the wake or funeral. She wanted to remember her daughter the way she was. It broke my heart to see her grieve. She kept saying, "I should be gone before her. Parents go first. Not my daughter!"

After the funeral we stayed in Connecticut for five days to visit with family. We had a nice time together, but were missing the vital person from our family that we loved so much. The day came when we had to say goodbye.

A few weeks later, I wasn't doing so well. I called my dad everyday to see how he was doing. "I'm just taking one day at a time," he said.

But me, I was not! I got angry with everyone and yelled at the boys. Even our cat, Meowie, stayed away from me. Every time she saw me coming she ran the other way. This was my cat—my baby—and I loved her. I knew she loved me too, but she was cautious. I was not nice anymore, something had changed. One day I called Pastor H from church and said I needed to talk with him as soon as possible. I figured if he couldn't help me, then I was going to check myself into a hospital to get help. I was seeking answers.

Geoff and I met with Pastor H that Saturday for a few hours. When we were done talking, Pastor H said, "Let's pray and ask God to help us."

"Well, you can pray all you want," I sneered. "I don't care what you say." Geoff and Pastor H got on their knees and started to pray. I sat in my chair shaking my head thinking they were idiots. God didn't hear them. God didn't care about us—or me! Then suddenly I heard myself say, "They are here!"

They stopped praying immediately. "Who is here, Pati?"

"Jesus is here. And He has my mother."

"Do you see them?" they asked.

I looked at them, like they were crazy.

I did not see them or hear a voice from God, but felt in my heart he was saying,

"Let her go, Pati, I have her." When I said that Geoff and Pastor H, they said my face went from a look of meanness, to the look of calmness. I sat up and felt better about everything. Geoff kept looking at me in amazement. Before we left, Pastor H prayed with us. I can't explain what happened to me that day, but I knew that my mom was in Heaven with Jesus. When we arrived home Meowie jumped onto my lap!

My dad was hurting so badly that he checked himself into a psychiatric hospital to get help. When I found out, Geoff and I went to the hospital to see him. I couldn't believe it. My father was a neat man—nothing out of place, clothes, house, and garage. Everything he owned was perfect. That was Dad! But the day we went to see him was a different story. He looked like a train wreck. His hair was a mess and looked like it had not been combed in weeks. He was wearing two shirts, both buttoned wrong. He had on two different colored socks, and hadn't shaved in weeks. My heart broke. He was a broken man—a sad man in pain. He kept saying, "I miss Mary, I miss Mary."

I went to see his doctor. "What can we do to help him?" I asked. The doctor suggested, maybe shock therapy. I was very upset and told him if they even touched him with this "shock therapy" thing, I would sue him and the hospital. The days I couldn't see him, the hospital let other people in to visit. My dad began talking to a real estate agent about the possibility of selling the house. I guess she found where he was—I surely did not tell her! She went to the hospital to have him sign papers to put the house up for sale. When I found out about it I was very upset. Thankfully, Dad hadn't signed anything.

I instructed the hospital that they were not to let that real estate agent in to see him under any circumstances. ANY!! I talked with my brothers more often and we decided Dad needed to be back in Connecticut. Dad liked the idea of going back home. We knew he wanted to be closer to Mom, and Florida was not it. My brothers and their families lived in Connecticut.

We did sell the house rather quickly, getting less for it than it was worth. We knew if we sat on it, Dad would get more money. We agreed getting Dad back to Connecticut was more of a priority than money. At first Dad was upset the house went for so little. He wanted to give the money to my brothers and me. We told him we didn't care about the money—only him! So we finished packing him up. My dad, Geoff, the boys and I walked through the house together. Dad told me how much Mom loved this house. She had everything she ever wanted—a beautiful home and a lovely yard with palm trees, a built-in swimming pool, enclosed screened porch and master bedroom with a big roman tub. The house was open and very airy—a wonderful Florida home.

"Dad, why don't you walk around the house one more time without me and say your goodbyes," I suggested. "I'll be waiting outside with Geoff, Michael and Geoff Jr." When he came out of the house, it was obvious he'd been crying. He tried to be strong.

The plan was that I would drive Dad back to Connecticut, stay a few days and then take a plane back to Cape Coral. So Dad said goodbye to Geoff and the boys. I said goodbye to my sons and husband and told them I'd see them in a week. When we got into the car, Dad kept asking me to stop. Then he'd turn around and look at the house again. Finally I said, "Dad, we are going now. Okay?" He smiled at me.

We had a wonderful time together. It was a great bonding time driving back home to Connecticut. Dad told me, with a sad look on his face, how happy he was to go back home, but it was going to be very hard living back there without Mom. I stayed in Connecticut for a few days to visit my brothers and their families. My dad found an apartment near my brother Tony.

When I returned to Cape Coral, we started to have financial problems. We sold our house and moved to Jacksonville in a two-bedroom apartment. Geoff got a job working with an air conditioning company in Jacksonville. Our Pastor in Ft. Myers told us of a church in Jacksonville and said maybe we could check it out. When we got to church that Pastor H suggested, Geoff leaned over to me and said, "This is the church!" I totally agreed with him. We joined the church.

Geoff was doing well at his job. My job was not bringing in enough money, so I got a better job. I was hired as office manager for a local department store. It lasted one year. One of the girls I worked with liked my job more than hers. She had some pull with upper-management, so I was let go.

VI

30 MORE MINUTES

On July 4, 1993 we received a phone call at 1:30 in the morning. I was half asleep and Geoff was sleeping. A woman was calling. I was not really sure what she wanted and told her she had a wrong number. We tried to go back to sleep. . A few minutes later the phone rang again. I picked up the receiver. "Look you have the wrong number!"

It was a man's voice. "Is this Mrs. Adams? Do you have a son named Geoffrey Adams, Jr.?" Then I heard, "This is Ken, the Chaplin at University Medical Hospital. Your son has been in an accident."

I woke Geoff and threw him the phone, "Geoffrey has been in an accident!" I got dressed and tried to wake Michael. He wouldn't wake up. I screamed, "Michael, your brother has been in an accident. Get up!!" I told Geoff I couldn't get him up. I tried several times, but he wouldn't wake up.

"We have to leave," Geoff said. I felt bad leaving Michael behind, but Geoff said he would call him later and come back and get him.

We got in the car and prayed. I asked, "Did the chaplain say anything else?"

"No," he said. "Just get here as soon as soon you can.'"

We flew to the hospital. Normally it takes 30 to 35 minutes to get there. It took us 15 minutes! We couldn't stop praying, "Dear God, after all we have been through with him, please don't let him die!"

When we got there, it was a nightmare! It was so busy— people bleeding, people lying on the floor— it was sick! We walked up to the window. They asked if we were Larry's parents. "No, we are Geoff Adams, Jr.'s parents."

"Sit down. We'll be right with you," an annoyed looking nurse snapped.

I sat there for two minutes, then went back to the window. "If I do not see my son, I am going to start screaming."

"What is going on?" the nurse demanded.

"Chaplin Ken called us," I said, trembling. She immediately took us to another room. I told her I could not just sit there—I wanted to see my son.

She brought us down the hall to a much quieter place, but as she walked with us, she told us that Geoff Jr. was in a car accident and the driver died on impact. Another boy was in critical condition and in surgery. "You'll be able to see your son in a few minutes. His wounds don't look too serious." Larry's parents were waiting in the room when we arrived. We started to talk and learned we all got the same information but they said their son, Larry, was life flighted in. A few minutes later they were called away.

Hours later a doctor came to find us. He told us our son needed surgery. "Doctor, we've been waiting for hours to see him."

"You can see him, but only for a few minutes," he said. We followed him down the hall and walked into a room with many beds.

"We are here to see our son, Geoffrey Adams, Jr."

Coldly, a nurse pointed and said, "Over there." I kept thinking about Michael. Why would he not wake up?

As I walked toward the bed I looked at Geoff. "I can't do this!"

"Pati, you can do this. You've been pitching a fit to see him."

"That's not Geoffrey. That's a black man!" Geoff motioned for me to come closer. And yes, it was our son. He was covered in mud and blood. They never cleaned him up. He was lying on the board they brought him in on—his neck still in a brace. His face was puffy and one of his eyes was swollen. But he was awake.

"Mom? Dad?" Geoff told him we were there. When I walked up to him, my heart crumbled. I didn't want him to see me crying, so it took every ounce of energy I had to smile.

> Memories of his childhood flooded upon me—his first tooth, his first step, the time he and his brother Michael cupped my face with their little hands and said, "Mommy I love you," and his first cry when he was born.

I was drifting back in time, but the sounds of the machines in the Emergency Room, brought me to the present. I looked at Geoff Jr. and saw those hands, now covered in blood and mud. I started to cry. I touched his face. He touched my hand and cried, "Jake is dead! He didn't see the car!" He asked if his other friends were okay. We told him they seemed to be okay. But we knew different.

We walked with the nurse and hospital attendees, as our son was wheeled to the elevator. We prayed over our son and told him that Jesus Christ was with him and not to be scared. We assured him that we loved him and would see him after surgery. We had to pray quickly. Geoff Jr. started to cry, so that made me cry even more. I reached out, touched his face and gave him a kiss. They wheeled the bed into the elevator. We stood there and watched the doors close. I fell onto the floor weeping. Geoff picked me up and walked me to the waiting room, then called his parents. It was about 7:30 in the morning.

"Let's go get Michael!" Geoff told me to stay and he'd go get him. He called Michael and said he was on his way.

The first person I called was my Sunday School Teacher, Jean. I told her what happened and the hospital where we were. She prayed with me over the phone and told me she would get the word out. I called my brother Tony and asked if he would call Dad. I knew if I heard my dad's voice, I would break down. I didn't want him to hear me like that. Tony told me how much he and his family loved us and said they'd be praying. I asked him to call Robert for me.

Geoff arrived with Michael. He was very annoyed with me for not trying harder to wake him up. From that point on, he never left our side. I hugged Michael a lot. Around 9 o'clock some of the folks in my Sunday school class showed up to pray with us.

I was overwhelmed with the love these people had for us. It was a little after 11:00 o'clock when the doctor came to talk to us. I felt like my heart was going to beat out of my chest. The three of us held each other—Geoff held onto me, I held onto Michael. The doctor told us Geoff Jr. made it through surgery. They had to repair his liver, spleen, stomach and kidneys. He was bleeding internally for six or seven hours. He said that if they waited 30 more minutes, he would have died. I took a deep breath and closed my eyes. "30 more minutes, 30 more minutes and my child would have been dead!

"Thank you, Jesus, for saving his life!" I prayed. Everyone else cried, as they thanked

Jesus for saving his life. We thanked the doctor. He told us we could see Geoff Jr. later. He would be in recovery for a few hours, depending on how he was doing. We could see him once he got a room.

Larry's dad came down to see us around noon. He asked about Geoff Jr. We told him he was just out of surgery and in recovery and we should be able to see him later. As we were talking to Larry's father, I sensed something was wrong. We asked how Larry was doing. Larry's dad was shaking as he told us that his son just died. I was in shock, I told him how sorry I was and I hugged him. Geoff hugged him, too. My Sunday school class witnessed this whole thing. We gathered around and prayed for him, his family and for his son.

I saw the pain in the eyes of Larry's dad. His pain was so real and haunting. I told him to call us if he and his family needed anything.

My Sunday School class prayed with us and then had to leave. I was overwhelmed by the compassion and love for my family. It showed me more about the love Jesus Christ has for us.

Later on when Michael, Geoff and I saw Geoff Jr. he opened his eyes and smiled. I reached over and kissed him on the forehead and told him I loved him. So did his dad and brother. He looked up at us and whispered, "I love you, too." When I heard him say that I cried. Then I cried for the parents of Larry and Jake whom I knew would never hear their sons say that again.

A week later, Michael and I went to Larry's funeral. Geoff Jr. couldn't go. The doctors wouldn't let him out of the hospital. He was extremely upset. During the service, I held onto Michael's hand, realizing how blessed I was to have two wonderful sons. I told Michael how much I loved him and prayed he would make right choices for his life. After the service we stopped by Larry's parents' house. Some family members stared at us. We knew they had questions we could never have answered. Maybe it was my imagination. Larry's parents were very sweet to us and said they would like to see Geoff Jr. when he was out of the hospital. We told them we would be praying for the family. As for Jake, his parents came down from Michigan and he was buried there.

My Dad told me he wanted to see all of us. So three months later, he paid for us to visit with the family in

Connecticut. Everyone was happy to see Geoff Jr. He showed off his scars. They were amazed how he survived the accident. They wanted to know what happened. So Geoff Jr. told them.

"Jake came by to hang out with us and some friends. He asked us if we wanted to go to the beach. Larry was getting into the front passenger seat. I told him, I didn't do back seats. So Larry got in the back and sat behind Jake.

"I was in the passenger front seat. Jake was driving. Larry was sitting behind Jake in the back seat. George was sitting behind me in the back seat. Jake didn't appear drunk, but he did stop and buy beer.

"Then Jake started driving fast. When we got onto Jay Turner Butler Boulevard, he was booking. He got off the Hodges Road exit and by that time everyone had put on their seat belts. We were all screaming at him to slow down.

"Then I got scared! The more we screamed at Jake, the faster he seemed to drive. As we approached the intersection of Beach and Hodges, I looked left. I remembered my Dad telling me that would be the car that would hit you first. But Jake was looking to the right, and he never saw the truck coming at us.

"I looked at the speedometer. We were doing 110!

"I yelled, 'We are all going to die!' The next thing I remember, I was hanging upside down, covered in mud and bleeding. But I was still in my seat!

"George told me the car flipped over three times and every time it did, my head flew in and out of the window. I felt warm all over. Jake's seat was on top of me. And Jake was still sitting in the seat. I don't think Jake knew what hit him. He was dead on impact.

"The car went through four lanes of traffic before we landed upside down in a ditch. I heard a lot of gurgling and didn't know what it was. I prayed and asked God not to let me die. I saw red flashing lights and heard sirens.

"They had to cut me out of the car with the 'Jaws of Life.' It was very windy and I thought I heard a helicopter.

"There was a very sweet, gentle, woman's voice I heard during the ride to the hospital. I couldn't see her, I think it was because of the blood and mud on my face, but I asked her not to leave. She said she wouldn't and told me I would be fine.

"Later in the hospital, I asked the nurse to find out about the lady in the ambulance, because I wanted to thank her. The nurse called to find out what ambulance brought me in that night. They checked their records and told her that there were only two men in the ambulance that night— no woman on duty!

"I think God heard my cry and saved me and sent a guardian angel to watch over me."

When I heard that, I knew God was taking care of him and watching over him. After Geoff Jr. told us what happened, everyone agreed.

Before we left for Connecticut to visit with family, we went to the place where they brought the car. I couldn't believe my eyes! How could anybody survive this accident? The driver's seat was on top of the passenger seat like Geoff Jr. said it was. The top of the car was crushed to the seats. The inside of the car was covered in blood and mud. As I stood there looking at it I wondered why I was looking at this. Two precious kids died in this car.

But it was a reminder to me that God is a great God—and not to take life for granted. It was a miracle that my son and his friend George survived.

VII

A MILLION PIECES

We noticed that Michael was different and actually liked going to church. We found out later that one night Michael knelt down next to his bed and trusted Jesus Christ as his Savior. Geoff and I were so happy and wondered what God had planned for his life. Michael told us he wanted to go on Missions trips. We saw him growing in his faith and were blown away by his knowledge of the Bible. He really got plugged into the high school ministry and choir at church. Geoff and I loved to see him singing on Wednesday nights. We knew Michael was being called for some type of ministry.

I found a temporary job with a local phone company where I worked for more than a year. I had a lot of friends, but one in particular made on impact on me. Terry was gay and very proud of it. We had long conversations about God and Terry's lifestyle. I told him, "God created Adam and Eve—not Adam and Steve," but we had very civil conversations each day on the subject. We never put each other down. Terry told me one day, "You know, Pati, I really like sitting next to you during our meetings."

"Do you like me or something?"

"Oh no, not that way! Just friends! You're the only person I ever met who calls herself a 'Born Again Christian' and doesn't put me down."

I smiled. "That is what Jesus would want me to do."

A few months later, I felt God tugging on my heart to give Terry a small Bible. But that wasn't all. I highlighted the whole first chapter of Romans and gave it to him. Ten minutes later my boss told me she wanted to see me in her office. When I got there, I saw the Bible I gave to my friend. I asked, "What are you doing with this?"

"Terry gave it to me, and he was extremely offended."

At first I was upset Terry didn't come to me first. Then I realized what was going on. My boss said, "Pati, you just might lose your job for what you did."

"Why?" I asked.

"I am sure you know the company is worried and already has people looking into this matter." She straightened a few papers on her desk. I just sat there with my eyes wide open. She told me that, unofficially, she was a Christian and applauded what I did. Officially, she had to comply with the company's position. "Don't speak with anybody about this until you talk with me again."

By the time I returned to my desk, the whole office knew what was going on. Some people laughed, some made rude comments. During lunchtime my co-workers snickered at me and called me a "weirdo." I knew this was what Jesus must have endured. Thoughts came crashing back to the cruel things kids said to me when I was a kid.

A few weeks later my boss called me into her office and said the "higher up" management said that I had to be "let go." She said he was offended with what I did and that I did it on company time. I packed up my things and was escorted out of the building. As I walked by Terry's desk, I stopped. He was reading a book and had no customers.

"Terry, I know you hear me and I just want to tell you that you are still my friend. Everything I told you about Jesus Christ is the truth. He loves you and I do, too. I pray you will remember the words I told you. Even though I probably will never see you again, I pray I will see you in Heaven." He just kept reading his book, but I knew he heard me.

After I was escorted out of the building, I walked to my car and put my things in the back seat. I got into the car and let the tears flow. Observers probably thought I was crying that I lost my job. That was the furthest thing from my mind. I was crying for my friend and his soul.

When I got home that night I cried on Geoff's shoulder. Here I was with no job, and we needed me to have a job. I felt desperate. "Now what?" I asked rhetorically.

My father-in-law had just applied for a job in the data entry department at our church. He realized that he was way too old for the job, so he told me about it. I applied— and got it. I was unemployed for only three days! God sure does move!

Things seemed to be going pretty good at the Adams household, but not for long. Geoff Jr. said he needed to talk with us about something. He didn't want Grandpa Adams around while we talked. We agreed, but wondered what was going on. The next day he and his girlfriend came over to tell us that she was pregnant. Pregnant! Geoff and I each took a deep breath.

I said, "All the stuff you've been through in the past year! I thought you were going to college and do something with your life—not this! I can't believe this is happening." He sank into his chair as we talked. It took a lot for them to come and tell us. I was going to be a grandmother! We talked for a bit and asked what they planned to do. They said they were thinking about getting married. A month later they were married. Our family was very excited as we waited for the new baby to arrive.

My wonderful husband was getting very tired of working with air conditioning. One day as he worked on an air conditioner he was extremely hot and noticed he wasn't sweating. He started to climb down a ladder, missed the last three steps and fell to the ground. He got in his truck to get cooled down and something to drink. He prayed, "Lord, if you get me out of this air conditioning business and back on the railroad, I will go anywhere you want me to go."

A few weeks later, Geoff had a call to fix an air conditioner at the Union Hall for Locomotive Engineers—Railroad! After fixing the problem, he asked the man signing his paperwork, "How do you get a job on the railroad around here?"

The man said, "Well, it so happens that the man you need to talk to is here." He pointed to a gentleman seated behind a desk on the other side of the room. Geoff spoke with him for a few minutes.

"Would you be willing to move if you were offered the job?"

Geoff smiled. "I believe so, but I will have to talk it over with my wife."

"There is a test in Ohio in one week, if you're interested," he was told.

Conversation around the dinner table was lively that night! Geoff told us what happened. He said, "I may have a chance to get back on the railroad, but it would be in Ohio."

I said, "Ohio!" Then we talked about the possibility of a new job back on the railroad. We'd be able to put Michael through college! So we prayed about it. Geoff called the guy back to let him know to put his name on the list for the test. The following week Geoff was on his way to Ohio.

A few days after he got back home, he received a call asking him to come back for a second interview. I told Geoff I wanted to go with him, so we drove to Ohio.

We got to Ohio and he had his second interview. Geoff felt it went well. We stayed a few days, looked around, and then headed back to Florida. We did a lot of praying and a lot of talking. We talked about Michael going to school, how much it would cost to move, and Geoff, Jr.—newly married with a baby on the way. It was a lot to digest, especially for me. I felt sick in my stomach—and sick in my heart. I thought I was a strong person, but I felt like my life was coming undone. My life was about to change—again!

Back in Jacksonville, my heart began to feel empty. Geoff Jr. left and got married, Michael was in high school.

And we may be leaving our home to go to a place where we knew nobody! Three hours after we got home, the phone rang. It was the railroad.

Geoff picked up the phone. We stood there listening. After a few minutes he told the person on the other end, "Hold on." He pulled the phone away from his ear. "It's the railroad calling. They're offering me a job. What should I tell them?" We looked at one another. "Pati, it's up to you, honey."

I took a deep breath. "Okay, let's do this."

Geoff smiled and turned back to the receiver. "Yes," he said, "I will take the job." He got more information and hung up the phone. He sat down and took a long gulp of coffee. "Well, I have to be in Ohio in two weeks."

I thought, "Boy! This railroad works quickly." As Geoff prepared to leave in two weeks, I had to prepare my heart. Allan, one of Geoff's good friends from church, told him he thought it was a big mistake. "I think you need to pray about it some more and wait a little while longer."

Geoff heard Allan's heart but he said, "God is giving me the opportunity to make more money to send Michael to college and help my family."

Allan argued. "God would not split up a family for the sake of money."

I talked with Allan's wife, Maria. She understood what her husband was saying, but also understood the need to put kids through college. "Maybe," she said, "something wonderful is going to happen with this move!" I really loved talking with Maria. She was soft spoken, and you could see Jesus Christ in her. We loved their whole family,

Allan Jr, Tiffany and Vinny. They were our best friends and we were going to miss them.

A couple of days before Geoff was scheduled to leave, he was packing and I just wanted to scream, "Stop packing! I can't do this!" I sat on the end of the bed, watching him pack and it hit me that he was really leaving for a job. I could see it was just as hard for Geoff as it was for me. We knew Michael wanted to go to college—and we would sacrifice for him. So here it was, the day Geoff was leaving. I tried to be strong, but my feelings and emotions got the best of me. I fell apart. Geoff held me in his arms. I never wanted him to let me go. My heart was being broken into a million pieces.

I touched his face, his eyes and hugged his neck again so I could remember how he smelled. This was all I had to hold onto until I saw him again. Geoff Jr. came over to say goodbye. Geoff's dad and Michael were there. Geoff's mom was not with us. She was diagnosed with breast cancer the year before and passed away in 1994. Geoff packed the car, gave everyone kisses and hugs, told us how much he loved us and how much he was going to miss us. He got into his car. My heart felt like it dropped out of my body. I was weak and scared. He backed out of the driveway and I watched him go down the road until I couldn't see him anymore.

I needed to be alone for a while. I went into our bedroom, fell onto the bed and cried for hours. I held onto Geoff's pillow—the one I told him he could not take. I needed something to remember him by.

A few hours later the boys knocked on my door to tell me dinner was ready. My wonderful father-in-law cooked dinner for all of us. I couldn't eat much. I sat at the dinner table looking at Geoff's empty chair. My strength had to come from God now. I knew He was right there with me. I picked up our Bible and flipped through the pages. I found a verse that got me through the following months—Proverbs 3:4-5. "Trust in the Lord with all of your heart and lean not onto your own understanding. Acknowledge Him in all thy ways and He shall direct thy paths."

So I dug into my job at the church, came home, had dinner with Michael and my father-in-law Mal, shared the happenings of the day. Michael gave me a few Christian tapes. I put them in my Walkman and walked around the neighborhood each night after dinner. This was my time with God and I started to believe that God was going to do great things in my life and our family's lives.

Geoff called me at work. I felt like a schoolgirl. The ladies in the office knew I was talking with Geoff. They thought it was so wonderful and very romantic. I met Geoff in Atlanta, Georgia for a weekend, while he attended his second school there. We knew our relationship was being stretched, but we felt that God was in on this whole move. We had a wonderful weekend together—and attended church together, too.

November rolled around and it was time to move to Ohio. That was the plan we made before he left. November he was out of school and working. Geoff's dad moved into a Senior Adult Living Center and Michael stayed back to finish high school. We allowed friends of Michael's to move in with him. We trusted Michael and knew he wouldn't let us down. Geoff Jr. and his wife were expecting a baby in

March. Geoff and I wouldn't be there. It was extremely hard to leave my two sons—especially the biggest time in our lives with a new baby coming. I talked a lot to God. "What the heck am I doing? What the heck are we doing? Our kids need us, and we are abandoning them?" I started to feel sick to my stomach! When I finished packing, the boys brought my suitcases out to the car. As I watched them, I shook my head and rolled those thoughts again in my mind.

I said goodbye to Mal. He was excited to be at the Senior Place. It was really nice. Michael prayed for of us and for me to have a safe trip. I put our cat, Bubba, in the car and gave everyone hugs and kisses. Suddenly this wasn't making sense to me. I pulled the car out of the driveway and waved goodbye. When I got around the corner, I almost had to pull the car over because the tears were clouding my vision. But I kept asking God to get me through this. Every time I cried, Bubba cried too, so I had to stop crying.

Bubba loved our family. We had him ever since he was four weeks old, when Geoff Jr. was in Outreach. I knew he, too, would miss the family.

But it would not be for long!

I stopped just past Atlanta for the night and sneaked Bubba into the hotel room, because they didn't allow pets. I called Geoff and the kids and Mal to let them know I was okay. Geoff was excited to hear from me. Everyone was praying for Bubba and me. That night I was mentally and physically exhausted. When my head hit the pillow Bubba jumped up with me on the bed and we both fell asleep. The next day was a very long trip. When we arrived in

Ohio there was snow on the ground. Geoff was so happy to see us.

Geoff and I worked at getting back to normal, but we missed our family. We hated that we were not going to be there for the birth of our first grandchild. I had to trust God that He was going to bring me through this.

When we received the phone call from Geoff Jr. telling us we had a beautiful new granddaughter, we were so excited! I could hear the joy in my son's voice. Our family was growing! I walked on clouds as I imagined my arms around that brand new little soul—my very own granddaughter! Months before, Michael called. He wanted to finish high school early at Florida Community College. We were so pleased he graduated at the beginning of March.

At the end of March 1996, Geoff and I drove to Florida to move Michael and Mal up to Ohio with us. When Geoff Jr. put that precious bundle from Heaven into my arms, I instantly fell in love. Her dad—our son—had tears in his eyes, he was so happy.

We stayed in Florida for a few days. I hated leaving Geoff Jr. and his brand new little family, but we had to get back to Ohio. As we said goodbye I realized my whole life I had been saying goodbye to people I loved.

Back in Ohio, Geoff's Dad settled into a one-bedroom apartment. Geoff, Michael and I moved into a two-bedroom apartment. I was happy that Michael and Geoff's dad were with us, but having Geoff Jr. and his family so far away was hard. One day we spoke on the phone with Geoff Jr and learned they were moving up north, to a little town an hour or so away from the Chicago area. But our excitement was short-lived. Geoff Jr. told us that he and his wife were not getting along.

Geoff and I prayed that God would help them through this and knew we had no control. Sometimes it is the hardest thing to let God handle things. Geoff Jr. called us in tears and said his wife wanted a divorce—but he wanted to try to save his marriage and family. We talked with him for hours. We suggested he visit with us for a few days—to get away and think clearly. His grandfather and brother wanted to see him. And Michael was leaving for Bible College soon.

Geoff Jr. made the trip to see us. "I don't want this divorce," he said over and over. He paced around the room, "I just want what you guys have—what Grandma and Grandpa's both had." He was near tears. "I know married people have problems, but you're just supposed to hang in and work it out." I poured him a cup of coffee and we sat at the kitchen table. "I can't stop thinking about what kind of life Heather will have, growing up without a dad."

"We're here for you, Geoffrey—whatever you decide. I wish we were wise and could tell you how to fix this. All we can tell you is to ask God to help. Let's pray together." It was a very hard road for us. I thought sadly about the granddaughter who would never get to know who we were, and how much we loved her. "God," I asked silently, "please help us through this."

VIII

GOD'S ROSES IN FULL BLOOM

Well, Michael went off to college. I knew he would be all right— it was just college. But to me it was a new journey for the whole family and more changes. The summer before Michael left for South Carolina, he decided to go on a mission trip to Thailand. We had friends that were missionaries there, so he was going to see them. I was worried about his traveling so far by himself. On other mission trips he was with a group. As I watched this young man pack his suitcases, my mind wandered back in time. I recalled him taking his first step, his excitement when he received his first bike. Michael told us he wanted to spend the rest of his life preaching the good news about Jesus Christ. I knew God had huge plans for our youngest son and I had better not get in the way. At that moment I started to let go of Michael and gave him to God. After all, he was God's child before mine.

We took Michael to the airport the next day. He flew to Chicago to Los Angeles, to Hong Kong, then to Chang

Rai. His total flight time was 32 hours. Michael called us when he arrived. He sounded tired, but was alive and well. Three or four weeks later, Michael arrived home, tired, but safely home.

Geoff Jr. called more often, saying he needed to talk with people that loved him. No one in his house was talking to him anymore. He lived about three hours away. I asked Geoff if it would be possible to move closer to him. Geoff asked his boss and found that he could work in the Chicago area. We moved to be closer to our son. We prayed a lot and asked God to help him. He had moved into a small apartment near his daughter, but he needed to save money and so, reluctantly, he moved in with us. A few weeks later he was served with divorce papers. That night he looked lost. He asked why he lived after that car accident while his friends died. "My life makes no sense," he complained, "it just has no meaning anymore." He moped around for weeks, but didn't realize our whole family hurt, not only for him, but also for our granddaughter.

Geoff Jr. is strong. He got through this. Work kept him busy. A few years later he met Karen. She was a very nice young girl. I could see Geoff Jr was really in love with her. Geoff and I liked her a lot and welcomed her into our family. They were married and in March of 2000 had a son. He was a precious little boy, just so cuddly, sweet smelling of baby powder. When I held him in my arms, I could not put him down. We loved him so much! He was our first grandson! When he started to smile, this beautiful boy could melt your heart. Karen had a daughter and son from a previous marriage. It was nice to see he was finally happy and having the family he wanted. We had our grandkids around us. They were fun to watch growing up. But in my heart I missed the special relationship I could have had with my first granddaughter, Heather. I prayed someday we would. I know God still answers prayers

Another mission trip was on the calendar for Michael. It was to Papua, New Guinea. He went with a Christian group. I felt much better about this trip. When Michael returned from New Guinea, he looked and talked a little differently. We couldn't put our finger on exactly what it was. We really got a clue when our phone bill that month was almost $750.00!

That was when and where he met Beth. One day I asked, "What's going on with you?"

"I met someone, Mom. Her name is Beth. She's really great and I like her a lot." I could see when he said her name, Beth, he lit up like a firefly. "I want to go to Pennsylvania and see her," he smiled. "Do you think I could take the truck?"

Geoff and I talked about it, and Geoff winked at me. We agreed. "Sure!" When he came back from seeing Beth, we knew our son was in love. I always wanted my boys to grow up, be happy and get married. I just didn't realize how quickly that day would show up. Michael told us he wanted to bring Beth to meet us.

By this time we had a beautiful two-story home in Chicago Heights. It was a typical 50s era American neighborhood. Houses were clean, neat, with fresh mowed green lawns and lots of flowers. We decided to put a little white picket fence on the corner of our driveway. It was our slice of Heaven.

The day arrived when Michael was to pick up Beth at the airport. We had never seen him so excited—and nervous. I don't think he slept a wink all night. Geoff and I peeked out the living room windows when they pulled up in the driveway. We were curious to get a closer look at the young lady who stole Michael's heart. She got out of the car and stayed very close to Michael while he got her bags out of the car. When she turned around I saw how beautiful she was—and so petite. Michael gave her a hug, and they stopped to share a few words. As they came into the kitchen, Michael puffed out his chest and smiled. "Mom, Dad, this is Beth." I knew immediately that she was the right one for Michael.

I hugged her. "Beth, we've heard so much about you. We are so glad you're here." Geoff walked over to Beth and gave her big hug too! Michael smiled from ear to ear.

Geoff and I liked her a lot. We could see that our son was happy to be with Beth. The week went by very quickly. It was time for her to leave and they were having a hard time with this. Geoff and I had to go to work the day Beth was to leave, so we told her to come back. We told her she was always welcome in our home.

It was snowing when Michael took Beth to the airport. When I returned from work, I saw a little pair of boots inside the front door. Beth and Michael were sitting in the living room with big smiles on their faces. I said, "What happened? Did they cancel your flight?"

"No. We got there too late and the plane was leaving the gate." I smiled, nodded my head and walked away. They were giggling like two little school kids. We knew Beth was the one for Michael!

Beth went home the next day. A week or so later, Michael was on his way back to Pennsylvania. It was cold and snowy and I was little concerned about him driving. "Michael, be sure to put on that warm coat," I worried.

"Mom, the truck has heat," he shrugged. "I'll be fine, but I will take my coat." When he got to Beth's house, he called and said he was okay but the heater stopped working about two hours from our house. It was a 12-hour drive one way! Michael told Beth there was no heat for the drive back to Illinois. She didn't care—she just wanted to be with him. She put a few comforters in the truck to keep them warm and they drove back to Chicago Heights. They stopped a few times, called us to let us know they were okay and on the way, and how much longer they would be.

Geoff built a fire in the fireplace and I made hot chocolate. We had a lot of blankets sitting in front of the fireplace ready for them.

Beth living with us was something Geoff and I prayed about. Something in our hearts knew she was already part of our family. Often when I arrived home from work, I'd find them reading the Bible together or just chatting in front of the fireplace. Geoff and I were not concerned about leaving them alone in the house. We knew God had a hand in this.

Michael told us he wanted to ask Beth to marry him and wanted our blessing. We were very pleased to give him our blessing. That night as I was getting ready for bed, I looked at the pictures on my nightstand. There they were—my boys at five and seven. As I looked at their beautiful faces—so young and innocent, tears filled my eyes, spilled over and rolled down my face. My little "Mickey Lee"—Michael—would be leaving soon. I knew this day would come, and dreaded it. But knowing the woman he would marry brought a smile to my face. I breathed a sigh of relief and offered a silent prayer of thanks to God.

Days later, Michael put on a suit and tie, cooked dinner for Beth and asked if she would marry him. When Geoff and I got home from work we heard the great news. Michael and Beth were engaged to be married!

They chose June 10th but realized that it would be hard to find a place for the ceremony on such short notice. They had no doubt God would help them find the perfect place. Beth looked through the Brides Book and found the Jacob Henry Mansion in Joliet, Illinois. It was a beautiful building, built in the 1800s for railroad magnate, Jacob Henry. Michael and Beth loved the place, but dates for June were not open. They put their names on the list and a few days later got a call. A couple scheduled for a ceremony on June 10th decided they wanted a Christmas wedding instead. Beth and Michael got their wedding date! Thank you, God!

Beth asked me to help her find a wedding gown. I was honored that she asked me and deeply, deeply touched. So I did what I do best—I cried—then I hugged her. God brought this precious young woman, Beth, into my life. Beth found the perfect wedding dress at the first place we went. It fit her perfectly. The only alteration was hemming the dress a few inches. Beth budgeted $200.00—and that was the price.

A few days before the wedding, guests arrived at our home. My dad flew in from Connecticut—my brothers and their families couldn't make it. Beth's friends drove from Pennsylvania. Michael's friends came up from Florida and Kentucky. After the wedding rehearsal we had a rehearsal dinner at our house. I sat back and watched my family hanging out having a great time, taking part in Michael's big day. My dad came to me. "They grow up so quickly, don't they?" I saw tears in his eyes and I knew he was wishing Mom were here. So was I!

We watched the "famous" family game of catch. Every now and then I heard, "Hey Mom, watch this." I watched them, smiled and cheered them on, remembering them saying that to me when they were little guys.

My dad leaned toward me and whispered, "Pati, you and your brothers used to say that, too." I knew that was what family was about—loving each other through thick and thin, always being there for each other. I looked at my soon-to-be daughter-in-law with her friends and knew that in 24 hours she would be part of the Adams Family. I knew the first day I met her she would be part of our lives.

That night the guys stayed in a hotel and the girls had the full reign of the house. We all got on our pajamas, painted our toenails and fingernails. It was great to have laughter of girls in my house.

The big day arrived and the morning was warm, sunny and beautiful, the birds where singing. It was a great day to get married. I did everyone's makeup, but I was so busy helping everyone else, I forgot myself. As I did Beth's makeup, my mind wandered into the future. What would her life be like with my son? Would there be grandchildren?

She looked like a fairy princess, just as sweet on the outside as she was on the inside. Beth and Michael wanted real flowers for the flower girl to drop on the bridal path, but money was tight. Before the day began, I went downstairs alone to get a cup of coffee. I looked out the window at my beautiful back yard and noticed one of the bushes on our little white fence had red flowers in full bloom for the first time ever! I tossed my cup in the sink and screamed for Beth and the girls. They came running down the stairs, thinking I must be hurt. What they saw was me—running outside screaming, "Get a bucket! Get pans! Get anything! Get out here!"

They stopped outside in mid-stride, amazed! Red and pink roses were in full bloom. Beth wept. "Oh, how wonderful! Thank you, God, for this wonderful miracle!"

"Okay, girls," I directed, "let's start taking the roses off the bushes." We must have looked like wild women in the backyard, picking roses off the bushes in our pajamas. We were careful to leave some blooms, so the bushes still looked pretty. We put the roses in a basket and ran back into the house. Later, when we were ready to go, we piled dresses and things we needed into the SUV. As I drove, the girls were giggling, crying, laughing—then tears again. I said "Makeup, Ladies—makeup!!" The beautiful blue sky was slowly turning dark. Silently I prayed that it would not storm. The car radio suddenly broadcasted a song just for Beth, "Going to the Chapel and We're Gonna Get Married!"

So I turned that sucker up! Everyone in the car belted it out at the top of their lungs. Boy, we were having fun!!

We got to the Mansion. It showered a little bit. Michael was late. He found out they did not have the English tie and silver vest he wanted—and there was no tuxedo. It did not show up for an hour and a half—and it was huge. He was extremely upset. Geoff Jr. was running late also. I was very upset! They both showed up at the same time.

Geoff came upstairs and knocked on the door where all the girls were to let me know Michael had arrived and everyone was ready. I gathered the girls and told them how beautiful they were. Together we prayed, "Dear God, thank you for this glorious day. Please take good care of Michael and Beth in their new life together." I gave Beth a kiss. "I'll see you out in the courtyard."

Geoff waited out in the hallway. When I left the room, I took the hand of my wonderful husband of 27 years and walked down the stairs. As the music started to play, we walked together down the aisle into a beautiful garden of flowers, trees, family—flowers and friends—and more flowers— where this wonderful wedding was to take place.

The music started for the bridesmaids and the flower girl who was spreading those miraculous rose pedals on the ground, the ones God gave to Michael and Beth for their wedding day. As I looked at Michael's face, I had no doubt that boy was just plain in love. It was the same look Geoff had on his face on our wedding day.

My heart was happy, but as I looked at him, I felt the door closing on a very big part of my life. No longer would Michael be the little boy that used to cling to my leg when

I had to go to work. No more would I see him clinging to the windowpane and see his little mouth calling me, "Mommy!" as I pulled out of the driveway to go to work. With mixed emotions I realized it was Beth's turn to have our son. My heart was bobbing back and forth as I looked at Michael and then Beth. They repeated their vows and looked so happy—and I was happy for them. I wondered where they would live. I knew he wanted to finish school.

Then I saw Geoff Jr. standing up as best man for his brother. It's funny how a mother's mind jumps from child to child. I turned my thoughts to my oldest son. What was going on with his family and his life? He and his wife looked so wonderful! What was God going to do in our lives? My boys looked so handsome and I thanked God for them!

Then quietly I slipped my hand into Geoff's and squeezed hard to let him know how much I loved him. He returned the squeeze. Then I touched my dad's hand to let him know that I loved him.

I heard the deep voice of the Pastor. "….I now pronounce you husband and wife." Then to Michael, "You may kiss your bride." They kissed in front of God and everyone. The majestic notes of the processional filled the air. Then the brand new Mr. and Mrs. Michael Adams turned around and walked down the aisle. Their faces were as I imagined! Love was in the air!!

After the wedding and dinner, Michael and Beth couldn't get out of there fast enough. Before they left, Geoff Jr. and Michael's friends soaped up the truck to let everyone know they were newlyweds. There was much commotion and people saying goodbye. We told Michael and Beth how much we loved them. Geoff just had to tell Beth he was not losing a son, but gaining a beautiful daughter. As Michael opened the truck door for Beth, he saw me standing there crying. He walked over to me, hugged me and told me he loved me. I choked out, "Michael, I love you so much. Have a wonderful life!" With that, he climbed into the truck. We all waved goodbye, and they zoomed away to their honeymoon in Daytona Beach, Florida.

Later, we all met back at our home. It was so good to sit and be with our son Geoff Jr. and his family, my dad, and friends of the bride and groom. We talked about the wedding and funny things that happened that day. By evening, people started to leave and my dad retired early to bed. Geoff and I sat there looking at all the wedding gifts, grandkids' toys still lying on the floor, balloons and streamers from the dress rehearsal dinner. All we could do was smile and thank God for our lives and the wonderful family we had.

Me in Kindergarten

Me in my rocker with bear, Milford, Connecticut

At grandma's house, I was 3 yrs old,
East Haven, Connecticut

Me at Grandma's house with my favorite
kitty cat, Christmas, 1954

Me on my new swing set, Milford, Connecticut

Geoff at 1 year old, Pecos, Texas.

Geoff riding his 1st "motorcycle" with
his Grandpa, Pecos, Texas.

Geoff riding his bike, Pecos, Texas

Geoff driving his car, Pecos, Texas

Our wedding day, Geoff and I, October 1973

Geoff and I, wedding day, October 1973

Geoff Sr with our son Geoff Jr. at Grandma's
house, Milford, Connecticut.

Geoff Jr. and dog Tammy at Grandma's
house, Milford, Connecticut

Me and Geoff Jr. Christmas party, 1976

Geoff Jr. at Grandma's house, Milford, Ct., Happy boy!

Michael, happy boy wearing his
food, Milford, Connecticut

Michael at 5 years old, West Haven, Connecticut

Geoff Sr with Michael and Grandpa
Adams, Meriden, Connecticut

Me and Michael our house in West Haven, Connecticut

Geoff Jr. 3 years old, Michael 6 months,
taken at my mom's house, Meriden, Ct.

Michael and Geoff Jr. at the duck
pond, Milford, Connecticut

Geoff Jr. and Michael hugging, Milford, Connecticut

Michael and Geoff Jr. "Rocking Christmas Day", West Haven, Connecticut 1980

Geoff and Michael, Clinton Little League, Clinton, Connecticut

Geoff Jr. and Michael, our house in
Cape Coral, Florida 1989

Geoff Jr. and Michael in our living
room, Chicago Heights, Ill., 1999

Me and Geoff back together again, Milford, Ct. 1978

Geoff Jr., Michael and Geoff Sr. the
night we got back together, 1978

Me and Geoff, Middletown, Connecticut 1983

Geoff and me (yellow shirt) at the 1st annual
"Lost Lid Boogie", New Hampshire, 1981

Me and Geoff after the "Lost Lid Boogie",
back home in West Haven, Connecticut

Me and Geoff on his 1965 Harley Panhead
(foreground) on I-95 in West Haven, Ct.

Geoff and me on the Panhead again.

Me under the turnpike bridge, Clinton, Connecticut 1986

Me before the show, Norwalk, Connecticut 1986

Me on stage, 1986

Just me

Michael and Beth's wedding day, Joliet, Ill., 2000

Geoff Sr, Beth, Michael and me

Michael, me, Geoff Sr and Geoff Jr, June 2000, Joliet, Ill.

Me and Geoff

Geoff Sr on 1979 "Shovelhead" in our
driveway, Chicago Heights, Ill. 2003

Me and Geoff on the Shovelhead in Calumet
City, Ill. Taken by Beth, 2004

Me and Geoff on the '79 Shovelhead

My dad with his great-grandkids, Meriden,CT.

Geoff Jr. with Natalie (our granddaughter)

Michael, Beth and Kids

Me speaking at our CareNet banquet, University of
Connecticut, Storrs, Connecticut
"Photo by JMacht Photography"

Me excited about the babies saved at our centers!
UConn, Storrs, Ct.
"Photo by JMacht Photography"

Next time check my hair before I go on stage!
UConn, Storrs, Ct.
"Photo by JMacht Photography"

Guest speaker making me laugh at banquet,
UConn, Storrs, Ct.
"Photo by JMacht Photography"

Our children's shoes, Ryan, Stephanie and Timothy.
Shoes courtesy of "A Cry without a Voice"
(Rebecca Porter)

Geoff, me and the shoes that our three children will never
wear, after I spoke at Hickory Grove Baptist Church,
Green Cove Springs, Fl., 2014.
Photo taken by Cliff "Pappy" Lamson

IX

ROOMS WITH TOO MANY TEARS

So our lives went on—Geoff working on the railroad and me working at a department store, selling cosmetics. At this time, I was having some female problems. I was cramping, bleeding a lot, dizzy and had no energy. I called my doctor for an appointment. She examined me and said I needed a hysterectomy. She gave me some options. The first one was to do nothing. The second was to do a partial hysterectomy. She highly suggested the third one, a full hysterectomy. She told me that I was at a very high risk for ovarian cancer.

So in September of 1998, I had my surgery. A few days later they let me go home to rest. One leg seemed to hurt all the time. I called my doctor to let her know what was going on and she ordered a test. A Venus Doppler was done to look at my leg. Two blood clots were discovered. I was rushed to the hospital and had a six-day stay—with orders not to get out of bed. Still in pain from major surgery I had a few days before, I was in tough shape!

I was to have medication after the hysterectomy, but not with the two blood clots. I was on Coumadin for one year. Although I was told I could not go back to work for six to eight weeks, I chose to return around the sixth week. I tried full time, but my body was having none of it. I knew I needed to go part time, but the cosmetic company I was working for had hired me as Counter Manager for a full time position.

I talked with the Counter Manager for another cosmetic company, and she told me there were no openings for part time positions. I prayed. "Lord, You know my problem, I need a little help." Within in a month there was an opening for a part time position. The upper management decided they needed three part time positions filled. I was hired. I was very excited and happy that God heard my prayers.

The Counter Manager was really surprised that, all of sudden, there was a position open for me. She asked, "Do you have it in with God or something?" I smiled. Our household seemed to be getting back to normal, but what was normal?

Michael and Beth told us they were expecting a baby. So in May of 2001, Emily Adams was born. Geoff and I waited outside the birthing room, and heard that precious first cry of our grandchild. We cried and hugged each other. A few minutes later, Michael cracked open the door and showed us a little bundle of sweetness in a pink blanket. We entered Beth's room, hugged and kissed the brand new, proud parents. When Michael placed that little bundle from heaven in my arms, I fell in love.

January of 2002, Geoff Jr and his wife blessed us with another beautiful sweet grandson. He was a bundle of joy, smelling of baby powder and so cute—and I just loved him! Geoff and I were so thrilled for our son and his family. Everyone was excited with this addition of another Adams in the family.

The same year, 2002, God blessed Michael and Beth with another baby—a boy they named William. They wanted to have this baby at home so a mid-wife was employed. Beth had her checkup with the midwife and everything seemed fine. But one day after she left, Beth felt something was not right and called the mid-wife to come back. As the delivery commenced, something went very wrong. The baby was blue and not breathing— the umbilical cord was wrapped around his neck. Michael and Beth were devastated. The midwife told Michael, "Pray over your son—and pray like you never prayed before! Tell God what you want."

Michael prayed, "God, please breathe life back into my son!" With that, William took his first breath! Beth told me that, as she watched her husband pray over their son who seemed to have no hope of living, she saw a miracle happen right before her eyes! When Geoff and I found out about this, we wept and thanked God for our little miracle grandson—our little William!

2004 brought another Adams into of Michael and Beth' family, little Miss Abby! We couldn't believe it. She was a cute little bundle from Heaven. I was in Grandma Heaven! Another granddaughter, I loved it!

I was very happy to see both my sons married and happy. Michael and Beth were living in Louisville, Kentucky. Michael was in Seminary. Geoff Jr and his family lived right down the street from us, so we were able to see them frequently. It was wonderful to be able to see our grandchildren. But after a time, things took a turn. Things were not going so well with Geoff Jr's marriage and it started to fall apart. It broke my heart. I wanted to see my boys happily married with kids of their own. There was a great sadness in my heart, knowing my son and his wife were not getting along. We prayed they could work it out and stay together.

Geoff and I joined a church. Every Sunday the church bulletin published information about things that were going on at the church—ministries that could use the help of members. Each week I read about the same ministry—over and over again. Each time I said, "Not me, Brother! Let's move along."

I loved working at my job. I loved my customers. I loved working with my co-workers and liked my boss. I loved getting free makeup twice a year! Tell me, what woman would not want free makeup? I do!!!!

But something in my heart was nagging at me—the more I brushed it away, the more it came right back. I called the church and asked about that ministry I kept seeing in their bulletin each week. So I talked to myself, "Okay, Pati Adams, now you have the number. What are you going to with it, Miss Smarty Pants?" I called and asked if they had any job openings. Why I asked, I don't know. I had no idea what they did—so why did I ask? Again I don't know.

Then the lady on the phone said, "As a matter of fact we do," and told me what they did.

Then my heart dropped and I gulped, "What do I do to apply?" She told me to hold on a minute. Sixty seconds later, I was talking with the Executive Director. She asked if I could come in for an interview. I made an appointment

A few days later I sat in front of the Executive Director of a Crisis Pregnancy Center. She asked about my past and how I came to Christ. We talked—okay—I talked for more than an hour! For some strange reason, I couldn't stop talking. She seemed very interested and had me fill out an application. She told me to pray and said she would call me in a week or two. When I got home, I started to think about the money and time difference. The next day I called and talked with the Executive Director.

"I don't know if you plan to hire me, but I don't want the job," I said before she had a chance to say anything. I was just about to hang up the phone.

"Pati, are you sure?" she asked quietly.

"Yep! And goodbye." I told myself it was okay. I talked with her and filled out the application. "Okay God," I prayed, half-heartedly, "I did what You wanted me to do. I am done."

Back at my job with the cosmetic company, I tried to forget about the Crisis Pregnancy Center. The nagging in my mind started all over again. Suddenly the job I loved became a drag—the hours felt wasted. Working on Sunday became an issue. I began to dislike my customers, and found fault with my boss. I still liked my co-workers. I knew something was up when I didn't like the free makeup anymore! I talked it over with Geoff and his advice was, "Keep praying about it and God will show you what to do."

This went on for three or four months. I felt God nudging me back to the Crisis Pregnancy Center. I told myself I didn't know how to talk to pregnant women. I didn't know if I even wanted to—and who did I think I was that I could do this? I wasn't trained for this. I didn't go to college for this. What did I think I was doing?

So I called them back to see if they just needed volunteers. When I did, I also asked if there were any paid positions. I had no idea why in the heck I did that! To my amazement there were. I thought, oh no, here we go again. I was about to get on this merry-go-round again! The receptionist told me to fax my resume to the Executive Director and someone would call me. Oh sure, someone would call me, I thought. They probably remembered me from the last time I called. I bet they thought I was some kind of a nut case.

I told Geoff what was going on. He typed my resume for me, but as he typed the cover letter, I noticed his hands were shaking. I stepped a little closer and peeked around to see tears streaming down his face. I put my arms around him and asked what was wrong. He just typed and cried. Then I looked at what he was typing. It was about our three abortions. He wrote, "If I could save one baby's life—and stop one girl from going to an abortion clinic— all my pain and sorrow would be worth it." That was the very first time Geoff said anything about the abortions—ever. We had never talked about it. I was in shock that Geoff had it on his mind, shocked that he could even type the word abortion, shocked that he really did care. And so shocked that he encouraged me to move forward with this job. I was speechless!

I secretly asked God, "Is there something to this?" Geoff and I exchanged glances. I sighed and headed to the store to fax my resume. Within 30 minutes of faxing it, the Executive Director called me for an interview. I was speechless.

The next day I went to my interview. I was very nervous and asking myself what the heck I was doing. There was a new Executive Director. We sat for nearly two hours. I told her of my earlier interview. She told me she heard all about it. I felt myself sinking into my chair. Yes—I was embarrassed. I told her I withdrew my application mostly because of money, and now I just wanted to do something for God. I felt it was not about money anymore. It was about what He wanted me to do. Maybe it was to help girls decide to keep their babies and not abort them. We talked a little longer. She told me to pray about the Center Director position. She promised to call me either way.

My family prayed for me to have this great opportunity. A month later I was told the position had been filled. There was another job, but it was a part time position. It was only 12 hours a week. The Executive Director asked if I would be interested. I told her I would be very interested. She said she would get back to me within the week.

I gave notice at the department store/cosmetic department. My boss asked where I would be working. I told her about the job and that it wasn't definite yet. I told her I felt it was what God wanted me to do. "You're leaving a job you do have, for a job you don't have yet? Why don't you stay until after Christmas, Pati? You'll be losing out on so much money. Besides, Christmas is only a few weeks away."

"I'm sorry, but no thanks. I need to do this." She shook her head and wished me luck.

I smiled, "Thanks, it's not about luck anymore—it never was."

I told my co-workers I was leaving and why. I got four different reactions from four different people. I told each one of them that I had three abortions and felt God was bringing me to the Crisis Pregnancy Center for a reason. One lady said, "How could you have had three abortions? I would never have guessed that about you, Pati."

The second lady shrugged her shoulders. "Oh well, what is done is done, time to move on."

The third lady never looked up as she organized the perfume bottles. "Oh well."

The fourth said, "It is okay, Pati. I am sure God forgave you." I blinked my eyes to hold back the tears. I was amazed at the different answers I got. It was the very first time I told anyone about my abortions.

A few days later I was offered the job and gladly accepted. My family was supportive and very excited for me. Deep down I was scared, but I knew God would see me through it. I started in December 2000 as a Client Service Director. Within three months I was promoted to Center Director at another Center location. I took it all in, got my training, still a little scared about what I was getting into—but trusted God.

I interviewed women who wanted to volunteer to be counselors and then we trained them. I saw young girls and women come into the Center being flippant about abortion. I realized that my story might make an impact on these ladies. What I failed to realize, however, was how telling my story would impact me. I got very close with my volunteers and they came with their stories and their hearts to help.

Some days we were so busy we didn't have time to talk to each other. But there were days that we could sit and chat with each other. We really got know one another. I told them, "If you ever get a client that is thinking about an abortion and you need me—come get me. I will drop whatever I'm doing to talk with them."

One of my Volunteer Counselors, Grace, was talking with a couple, Sue and Evan. When they came out of the counseling room, I was standing talking with another Volunteer Counselor, Carol. We stood there talking to this couple. I shared about my past three abortions, and how I was doing with the decisions I had made.

Carol shared that she was adopted and how it affected her life—that her mother had chosen life over abortion.

Grace told them she couldn't have kids of her own, so she and her husband adopted three boys. She shared the joys they experienced with their huge family.

"I guess we have a lot of big decisions to make," Sue and Evan agreed. "We'll let you know what happens." We prayed with them, and told them no matter what choice they made, we loved them and would always be there for them.

A few weeks later, they called Grace and told her they decided to keep their baby. We were so happy!

About eight months later, Grace and I were in my office when one of the Volunteer Counselors knocked on the door and said there were two clients to see Grace. They had a baby girl with them. We peeked out of my office and saw who it was—and almost tripped over each other getting out the door. Grace and I cried when we laid eyes on this precious little girl. We couldn't wait to hold her. Grace held her first. We both wished Carol were here to see them.

"Grace and Pati," the new daddy said, "because of what you told us, and then praying with us, we realized the pregnancy was more than we were thinking—it was a life." God gave us a huge gift that day. We knew we played a large part of the little life in our arms. That year God finally gave me a glimpse of what He wanted me to do for the rest of my life. It was to defend life, to educate women and men so they could understand how abortion hurts everyone.

Our Center had a ministry program that helped women deal with the pain and shame of past abortion(s). I knew in my heart I needed to do this, but something pulled me back. I kept telling myself I knew God had forgiven me. So why did I need to dig it all up again? I was already working and doing what God wanted me to do. So why this? Why now?

I signed up for a class and I didn't go. I signed up for another class and I was a no show there, too. One night the Director for the Abortion Recovery Program asked me a question. "Now Pati, don't get mad at me for what I am about to ask you. I know your biker background," she grinned. "Did you ever lose anyone in your family?"

"My mom died in 1991. My grandmother died in 1994. My mother-in-law died 1994. And my father-in-law died in 1999. So why are you asking me?"

"When your mom died, did you ever see her in a coffin?" she continued.

I was getting a little annoyed—no—I was getting very angry. "Where the heck are you going with this? And it better be fast. And yes, I did."

"Did you see her put into the grave?" she asked.

At this point I was about to pop her one. But I didn't. I said, "Yes."

Then she said, "Pati, so you wept for your mom. Did you ever weep for your three aborted babies?"

I stood there with my mouth open. I wiped away tears that started down my cheeks. "No, I have not done that."

"That is why you need to come to this program. You know with your being on staff, this is mandatory." I signed up for the next class. And I was there!

This program also dealt with miscarriages. Another staff member, Patti, went through this program with me. It was a hard 12-week program, but I made it though. Patti and I shared a lot of Twizzlers through that program—and lots and lots of tears. Because we went through this together, we knew we would be friends for life.

After the 12 weeks of this Post Abortion Program, I realized I had been carrying around the weight of guilt and shame for almost 25 years. Looking back at my life, seeing the mistakes—the decisions I made—were basically based on pain from my past abortions. I really had no idea how these abortions affected my life in such a powerful way.

God had been with me the whole time and now I felt as if my burden, chains, pain, shame and guilt was lifted from me and I was free. Going through this program, was one of the best things I ever did for my family and myself.

When I was at the Pregnancy Center another staff person I worked with was named Pat. She scheduled the Directors to speak at churches about the Centers. It was great to share with the churches, the stories of clients making decisions for life, but then the sad decisions of clients choosing abortion. Letting them know how each of these decisions affect not only the churches, families, but also the community. Pat really kept me hopping. We became fast friends. Her husband Ed volunteered at my Center. He spoke with male clients and was very good at what he did. Sometimes it was kind of funny and confusing to have three Pat's working at the Center.

As I became more involved at the Center, the volunteers shared with me some of their concerns for things that needed to be changed in order to better serve our clients. We wanted more accountability with our clients. We needed to give them a hand up—not a hand out. It is a program that clients go through when they have made a decision to parent their baby. They would come in each week. We'd have them watch videos on parenting and taking care of a new baby. Then we'd give them homework to take home and bring back for their next class. They could earn points to get items for their babies. The "higher-ups" at the Center told me they would love to do that, but it took a long time for things to change. I was asked to be patient. I brought this up every other staff meeting because I knew how important it was. I didn't what them to forget. I knew this was God's ministry—not mine, but I was getting frustrated. I asked them, "Can we at least try something?" I was told to be patient!

We had 12 Volunteer Counselors and between 50 and 60 clients per month when I started. These numbers grew to between 30 and 40 Volunteer Counselors, who saw 150 clients per month—give or take a month here and there. I worked long hours and got more volunteers so we could serve more clients. My heart was with what I called "the little lambs walking through our doors." One local church came in and renovated the whole basement for us. My Pastor and the church volunteers helped us with closets, shelves and bins, so we could store the baby clothes we gave to clients. The Center was growing by leaps and bounds. I asked for more staff help. My boss spoke with a few ladies, offered a position, but no one accepted. So they put the positions on "hold."

In their defense, they did send me a lady from another Center to help out with our busy days when they could. So I dug into what God called me to do. One night I was working with Terri, one of my Volunteer Counselors. We had a slow night and none of our appointments showed up. Around 7:00 p.m. we saw Shelly, a walk-in client who said she needed a pregnancy test. Terri took Shelly into one of the counseling rooms. Forty-five minutes later Terri came out to get me. She told me the test was positive and her client was not keeping this baby because she had no idea who the father was. She was living on the street.

Terri told me that she shared about the Gospel and Jesus Christ. She said the girl trusted Christ as her Savior, but still wanted to have an abortion. Shelly was happy about Christ, but now confused about the pregnancy. When Terri talked to Shelly about alternatives, like adoption, she would not hear any of it. Our volunteer asked if she would like to talk to her director. Shelly said, "I guess so."

As I walked through the door, I knew I had my work cut out for me. Shelly took one look at me and her body language screamed she didn't want to talk with me. She looked me up and down and gave me a lot of dirty looks. I ignored it. Something told me to move forward. I was going to tell her like it was. So that is what I did.

As I started to talk, she rolled her eyes and looked at Terri, "Is this chick for real?"

"You don't want to talk to me, do you?" I asked her.

"Honey, you have no clue about my life! You look like a little white church prissy mouse that nothing bad has ever happened to. So you have no clue, Honey!" I sat back in my seat. I shook my head and smiled. God was giving me the opportunity to really let her have it! There are some clients you can do this with, and some you cannot—God always seemed to let me know which ones they were. As I looked at this client, my past flew by me—all the drugs, drinking, wild parties, biker life style, getting beat up, my three abortions. This poor girl had no clue who was sitting in front of her. But I was about to let her know!

With love and compassion I said, "What you see is what looks like a 'white church prissy mouse.' But you never saw me taking drugs, drinking until I couldn't stand anymore— the biker lifestyle I lived! You never saw the pain I went through with my three abortions. You never saw my kids all screwed up from the lifestyle I was living— and a marriage taken to the brink of divorce." I assured her this "white church prissy mouse" wasn't so white a long time ago. Her body language changed. Her arms that were crossed were not any more. The look on her face changed. At one point she pulled her chair closer to mine. Then I said, "I'm not here to impress you or blow smoke up your butt. These are the facts. Take it or leave it—it's up to you!" I also told her that Jesus Christ had changed my life and the decisions that I make now, is to honor Him with my life.

At that point I believe Jesus Christ was doing a lot of work on her. I think she realized that I was not some "white church prissy mouse," but that I actually used to have a lot of stains on me. She started to cry. I was pouring my heart out and sharing my mistakes. I felt that earlier in her life she might have had an abortion.

She told me no one had ever been so honest with her. "I can't believe anyone would care enough to share their story with a total stranger," she said, drying her eyes.

"It was not a mistake that the guy you were with just dropped you at our Center," I said. "God brought you here tonight—to Terri and to me—and Christ brought you right to Himself. This was no accident." She kept looking at Terri and me with wonder and amazement, wiping the tears.

She shook her head. "God," she said, looking up to heaven, "I can't believe You would love me this much to send these ladies into my life!" Then we heard her whisper,

"Thank you, Lord." She said she would be willing to keep her baby if she had a place to go.

Shelly had no transportation. We called a couple places for her. I contacted a maternity home and they said they had a room, but couldn't get out to us until the next day. The person on the phone said, "If you can get her here, we'd love to have her."

Terri was willing to take her, but I told her, staff and volunteers couldn't take clients anywhere, due to legal issues that may arise. Terri felt she needed to do this. We told Shelly to wait in the counseling room, for a minute or two. I dragged Terri into my office and we prayed!! Boy did we pray!!! We asked God to please give the Center and us grace and mercy, because I was going to let Terri take Shelly to this maternity home. I felt in my heart it was what God wanted us to do. When we told Shelly, she started to cry. I asked if I could hug her. She gave Terri and me each a huge hug.

I called the maternity home to let them know she was on the way. They were very happy to have her and said they would take good care of her and the baby.

I called my supervisor to let her know what I just did and if anything should happen, it was on me. She was very understanding but told me not to do it again. She hoped I prayed about it before I made the decision. I told her I did— and felt God was in this. Sometimes we have to follow where God's leads us, and that is what we did that night. Our Center got very busy and I lost touch with Shelly. This should never have happened—but God had a plan.

About a year later, my supervisor decided to take the Center Directors on a field day to the Maternity Homes where we can send our clients. When we got to one particular home it hit me that it was where we sent our client, Shelly. I asked the Director of the home about Shelly.

"I remember her," the Director said. "You wouldn't believe what happened!" She told us every time they had meals together, she cautioned the other girls not to do what she was doing—prostituting herself. She told them about the problems that brought her to the maternity home. She was pregnant at almost 40 years old. The director told us Shelly also did Bible studies with the younger girls. Shelly went into early labor and had her baby boy at seven and a half months. She chose adoption. A pastor and his wife adopted him.

Shelly said she wanted to get her life back on track, go to school and make something of herself. She knew she couldn't give her son the good life he deserved. The Director showed me a picture of Shelly with her son before he was adopted. I couldn't stop crying. God allowed Terri and me to have a small part in this woman's—and this little boy's lives.

I knew that night when I told Terri to take the Shelly to the maternity home that God was in this. Boy! Was He ever!! I called Terri the next day. She was on her cell phone, and told me, "Hold on. I'm driving and I have to pull over." When I told her what happened she screamed—screams of Joy, and thanking Jesus Christ for taking care of Shelly and her baby.

When I started working at the Center, Volunteer Counselors sometimes worked alone. I told my boss I was closing a few nights until I could find some more volunteers. I knew it was the right way to run a Center—and the right thing to do. I told my boss I needed help as I tried to figure out the best way to stay open. We were in an area that really needed us to be open more hours. I asked Volunteer Counselors to switch days to nights and nights to days. Some even did a couple days. The regular Volunteer Counselors shift was three or four hours.

My boss told me if I had to work alone to be open—just do it! I couldn't believe what I was hearing. Being alone was unsafe. Geoff said he wouldn't allow me to work there by myself. The area had gang members and drug users. Working alone was never a good thing. I told the administrators about my concerns. The response was, "Are you afraid to be alone? Do you have some fear issues?"

That comment kind of took me back for a minute. "No, I don't have any fear issues," I said. "I just believe that no Volunteer, Staff, or Board Member should be at any Center alone—day or night, with the doors open." After a few minutes with no response, I asked, "Please, could I get some help from you guys?"

"You could lock the door, put up a sign telling clients to knock to be let in," I was told. "Then you could let them in to make an appointment and tell them to come back at a later time."

"If a client walks in those doors and wants a pregnancy test, I will not just make an appointment for them to come back," I replied. "I can't turn them away— isn't that why we are here? We are a Crisis Pregnancy Center! A woman at our door is in crisis at that moment—not tomorrow! If we don't take care of her when she comes in, she may go to an abortion clinic—and we know what happens there!" I was fighting a losing battle. I was not the victim—our clients were the victims. I tried to reason with them. "You know I was once one of these girls." I took a deep breath. "I can't believe I am talking with two Christian women who are telling me to do these crazy things. What is going on?"

They let me vent, then told me to do what they asked. I sat at my desk and cried. "God," I prayed, "did I just do something wrong here? I am displeasing to You, Lord? I need help, what am I going to do?"

As time went by, I tried to focus on what God had called me here to do. I asked more Volunteer Counselors to switch hours and days to help me out again. Some of them did. It seemed everything was okay, but it really was not. The Volunteer Counselors wanted to know why the Center was not doing more to help the clients. They wanted to know what was going on. I told them, "It's God's ministry. Let's keep helping the clients the best we know how."

X

TINY LITTLE SHOES

I tried to stay true to my position, and when the Volunteer Counselors had questions I answered them the best I knew how. But when I approached the leadership of the Centers, I was labeled a troublemaker. They never came out and said it, but I could tell by their actions, body language—and the words they were using. I was upset and frustrated about the whole situation, and I knew my relationships with some of the leaders were quickly fading away. It made me very sad.

Geoff and I talked about moving back to Jacksonville, Florida. We tried to sell our house, but it didn't sell. We prayed and asked God for direction in our lives. Geoff considered enrolling in Harley Davidson School in Orlando, Florida. At first I was not happy with the idea, but he was not happy at his job. I saw the worn look on his face. His body was wearing out with all the stress. He wondered if he was going to make it through each day.

As we prayed, we felt we needed to try harder to sell the house, and see and if Geoff would be accepted to the Harley School. We prayed—waited—prayed, waited some more. In March 2004, Geoff was enrolled. His classes were to start in February 2005.

Missy, one of my Volunteers Counselors was a real estate agent, so we asked her to sell our home. She was overwhelmed to be asked to handle the sale of the wonderful home that I loved so much. She had her Real Estate License for only a short time. I told her I wanted a Christian to sell our home. But down deep I was nervous about selling. It was not because of Missy. It was because I loved my house, and it was very hard. The homes in our neighborhood were homes like those in the 50s—safe and beautiful.

We sat on our porch as we signed the papers to sell it. I was not happy. "Geoff," I confessed through the tears, "I don't want to do this. Are we sure we're making the right choice here?"

Geoff took my hand. "Pati, didn't we pray about this? And didn't we both feel that God was leading us back to Florida?"

"Yes," I answered, wiping my eyes.

"Then sign the papers, Honey,"

A few days later we drove to Louisville, Kentucky for our granddaughter Emily's third birthday. Missy called and told us that she had put the sign up in front of our home. We had a wonderful time with Michael and Beth, Emily and William. She had a "Little Princess" birthday party and all the little girl guests were dressed in princess gowns. William was a Knight with a sword and crown. I loved being with my family and grandkids. So why, I wondered, was I moving back to Florida? Louisville was only a four-hour drive from Chicago Heights. As I realized it was a 12-hour drive from Louisville to Jacksonville, my heart started to grieve.

Five days after Missy put the sign in our yard, we had two offers on our home. We were amazed. I didn't know whether to be sad or happy. Missy dropped by after church to give us the details. The prospective buyers didn't have to sell their house. We could close in a month!

I sat on my beautiful screened-in porch to sign the papers and couldn't bring myself to sign them. Geoff asked, "Honey, what is wrong?"

I looked into his eyes and let the tears flow. This set Missy crying, too. I took a deep breath. "You know I prayed about this. We prayed about this. I know this is the right direction, but it's still very painful." I read the papers and signed them. I slumped into my chair and looked at the trees and flowers in my garden. "God will provide another garden with more flowers, more trees." Just then the wind touched my face. I felt God's presence. I-wished I could take my home and neighborhood to Florida. Then I realized how dumb and silly that idea was.

Grace, one of my Volunteer Counselors, asked what we planned to do after we moved out of the house. She knew Geoff wasn't going to start school until February. I told her we would, most likely, get an apartment for six months and move to Florida in January. "Oh, no! You guys need to come live with Bob and me," she said.

I thought she had just lost her mind. I smiled. "No way. We can't live with you guys. It's too long a stay!"

Grace wouldn't take "no" for an answer. She told me they had a huge house and sometimes had missionaries stay at their home. "We had a Pastor and his family stay at our house for seven months. Pati go home and tell Geoff—and pray about it!" So I did.

Grace told us we didn't have to pay to stay with them. I disagreed. "Grace, we can't stay there without paying you."

"Oh Pati, get over it! I won't take any money from you! This is time to save your money for the move."

I was dumbfounded. It was the sweetest thing anybody ever did for us. Geoff and I went to see Grace and Bob. We wanted to know the rules of the house—and where to park our car. On June 30, 2004 we moved in with Bob and Grace.

The last day of our move, I checked the rooms to see if we got everything. Memories flooded my mind and soul. My eyes filled with tears. I remembered the day we bought this beautiful home—how Geoff and I knelt in front of the fireplace and gave our home to God and thanked Him for it. We had so many memories from five years in this house.

I recalled our first granddaughter—Geoff Jr.'s daughter—coming to visit. She ran from her daddy's Mustang with arms out toward me, holding her little stuffed animal "Sheepie." She shouted excitedly, "Gamma!" That was the last time she would be in this house. I remembered two weddings in this house—Geoff Jr.'s wedding, then Michael and Beth's. Memories continued with Michael's proposal to Beth in front of our fireplace—all the grandkids.

Geoff Jr.'s son was a little bundle of joy! As he got older, he was like a whirlwind running through our house and up the stairs. When he didn't get his way, he threw himself onto the floor, just like his daddy did as a child. It was interesting to see Geoff Jr. handle his son. He had to contend with those big brown eyes and that huge smile. When they had another beautiful baby boy, he had so much energy it was hard to keep up with him.

Michael and Beth's sweet little Emily was born. We were so excited to be such a huge part of her life. I loved to hear her little cries—and the smell of baby powder that filled the upstairs bedroom. I remembered the day Geoff and I took Emily out for a walk in her stroller. As we turned the corner we saw our sons playing catch. Their wives and our grandson watched with interest. It was a beautiful summer day. Geoff said, "Honey, this is what it's all about—family!"

I came back to reality, wiped away the tears and finished checking the house. Every single room had so many memories. It was getting too hard. I went into the room where the grandkids took naps, now empty and bare. When I closed my eyes, I could hear the room full of laughter, a baby crying, see the little squeaky toys and smell the baby powder. I remembered being greeted with big smiles when I walked into this room to get my grandbabies up from their nap. I could see the arms outstretched for lots of hugs and kisses. We all knew this was the best room in the house. It got the best breeze from outside and warmth of the sun in the afternoon.

Then I heard Geoff calling me. I stopped, opened my eyes and saw the room that had been filled with the smiles and laughter of my grandchildren. It was now a cold, empty room. No more carpet, no stuffed animals, no more smell of baby powder— just a cold, empty room. The only thing that remained was the pretty wallpaper on the walls. I told Geoff I'd be right down. I brushed my hands over the walls. The smiles faded.

I walked down the beautiful staircase remembering the children sneaking up the staircase to play. I walked into the living room. "Are you okay?" Geoff held out his arms. I walked up to him and buried my face in his chest and wept. He wrapped his arms around me. "It'll be okay, Pati," he said, patting my back, oh so gently.

"God is sending us on a new journey now," Geoff continued. "And we're going to make new memories in Florida." I knew he was right, but the pain was very real. Geoff took my hand and led me over to the fireplace where we began our journey on Campbell Avenue five years earlier. We knelt down, bowed our heads and thanked God for this beautiful house He allowed us to buy. We thanked Him for all the wonderful memories that were made in this home and knew we would never forget them. We asked God to bless the family that would buy our home. We prayed their lives would be lifted up to glorify Christ—and they would see Christ in their new home.

As we ended our prayers we looked at each other and recognized the memories in each other's eyes. We hugged. I wondered if I would ever get through the day. We packed a few little odds and ends and walked through the kitchen. I gasped, "Oh the doorway, the doorway!"

I suddenly remembered the doorway that led to the cellar and how I charted my grandkids' heights and dates. I walked over to look at it. I touched all the dates, heights and names. I couldn't control my emotions. Geoff came over to me. "Pati, honey, you've got to let this go."

I blew my nose. "I know, I know, but can we cut the wood off the doorway and take it with us? I don't think they would mind."

He smiled and shook his head, "Pati, no. We cannot start taking the doorframe apart. The new owners would be very upset."

"I don't think they would mind. Besides, any woman would understand this!"

Geoff rolled his eyes. "Please, come on."

So my wonderful husband won this battle—but I knew he was right. When we got to the back door, I remembered those tiny little shoes all piled up next to the back door. I knew my family loved this house as much as we did. Geoff took me by the hand, turned around, looked back and together we said, "Thank you house, you served us well." With the turn of doorknob— and turn of the key— we walked out.

We were walking into a new chapter in our lives. We saw that our next-door neighbors, Deborah and Kerry were home. They came out and Deborah blinked away the tears in her eyes. "Is it time already?" We hugged each other. "You guys have been the best friends and neighbors anyone could have. We sure are going to miss you!" We laughed at all the times I let her son and Gina's son run through our back yard.

The yards were connected with no fences, just bushes here and there, so it was easy for them to play. Gina and her family were our other next-door neighbors. I told Deborah I enjoyed watching the boy's run and play, and when my grandkids came over, how it was even better. It was great, just like in the old days when neighbors looked out for each other.

Next we said goodbye to Gina and her family. I cried— again. Gina told me she'd miss the chats we had in the back yard and would miss me. We hugged goodbye. We promised we'd be back to see them.

I got in my car and Geoff got in his truck. As I backed out of my driveway for the last time, I took a deep breath, one more look at my wonderful home and said goodbye.

As I drove down the street, I wiped the tears from my eyes. I reflected on my life— the moves and changes, and all the people that have walked through my life since I was that little girl near the seashore. The memories that flooded my mind were so overwhelming I had to convince myself to think about something else.

I thought about how God had been with me every step of the way, even before I really knew who He was. That put a smile on my face. I was ready to see what He had planned next for my life.

XI

GRACE AND STITCH

When we arrived at Grace and Bob's home, we started a page in our lives with another family. I never had second thoughts about moving into their home—I knew God was in this whole thing. As we adjusted to new schedules, we didn't see Grace and Bob very much. By the time I got home from work, Bob was in bed, but Grace was up. Grace and I chatted about our day, our kids and our grandkids. Grace and I shared a lot of stuff from our lives and what we wanted out of life. We prayed a lot together, which we both needed. One thing I loved about Grace was her laugh. Every time I heard it, I couldn't help myself. I laughed.

We talked about my job and how stressful it was getting. I planned to tell my boss I was leaving at the end of the year. I wanted to let them know in plenty of time, so they could find a replacement for me. Grace told me to pray about it and God would let me know when and what to do. I did pray and asked God for guidance, but I felt in my heart it was time to tell them.

In August 2004, I wrote my resignation letter and asked for a meeting with both of my bosses. I was very nervous, but knew I was doing the right thing. When I walked into the office and we settled down to talk I told them I had news to share and gave them a copy of my resignation letter. I stated Geoff and I were making a life change, moving to Florida and my last day would be December 31st. I also stated I felt I had done a good job and was praying for a new Center Director. It was a pretty simple letter, short and to the point. They sat there with their mouths open, in total shock, like a couple of deer in the headlights. They stumbled over their words and took deep breaths. It looked like they were trying to collect their thoughts. They told me they would miss me very much and appreciated my resignation letter early, so they could start looking for a new Center Director.

Several times the Head of the Centers got up to hug me. "You'll be missed so much, Pati," she said. "You've done a great job in the four years you served as Center Director." My fears were washed away when I saw how they took the news. They asked, "We know you sold your house, so where are you currently living?"

"We're staying with Grace and Bob until the end of the year," I said. "I'd be happy to help you find and train a new Director. I can help with the Volunteers Counselors, introduce the new Director to the church pastors, church leadership and familiarize her with relationships that I built with local businesses." I was getting excited.

They agreed, but said they wouldn't start looking for a Director until mid-October—after the Annual Banquet. I told the staff I was leaving, and they were surprised. Each one got up from what they were doing to give me a hug. Each one of them had tears in her eyes. They all knew how much I missed Florida and told me they were going to miss me.

As the months went by, Grace and I had a great time together. Bob liked to play practical jokes and had a box of them. I think that is why he got the nickname, Stitch. One time he put ice cubes with a fake spider in one of my drinks, and freaked me out. I ran to the sink, spit out my drink! He'd come into the kitchen and smile with his "Billy Bob" teeth. When Grace and Bob laughed—even if you were not in the mood to laugh— it was infectious— you couldn't sit there without laughing. I loved it. They took several short trips leaving Geoff and me home alone.

My job got rougher as each day passed. My Volunteers Counselors asked me daily if anyone was hired. I told them the hiring was planned for after the banquet in October. They told me when there was no Center Director it was not good. I told them, "God will get a Director."

October was upon us. Geoff and I headed to Florida to check out apartments and the Harley Davidson School. Geoff Jr. called to tell us he just got a job with a railroad in Jacksonville. Geoff joked, "Do they need any more help?" I looked at him, mentally asking what he was doing.

Geoff Jr. said, "Yep, I think they need more help." A couple days before we left for Florida, Geoff Jr. called back and said that his boss was looking to hire another engineer.

"I'll get my resume together, and bring it along," Geoff said. On the way to Florida, we talked about having no insurance for the prescription medicine I was taking. We got to Orlando and stayed a few nights, looked at apartments and visited the Harley School. Then we headed to Jacksonville to see Geoff Jr. for his birthday. Geoff met with the railroad boss.

Our son thought it would be cool working side-by-side with his dad. He already went through two bad relationships, and had two divorces with children. He came to Florida to visit with a friend and ended up with a job. He hated to leave his two boys and his daughter. But the way the relationships were, it was very hard for him to stay. He told us, "All I ever wanted was to be married, work hard for my family, have a nice home, go to church, go on vacations and love each other. I just want what you guys have, what Michael has and what my grandparents had." I prayed for God to show him the way.

Geoff was offered the job on the railroad. Our journey to Orlando was over—and our journey to Jacksonville began. Geoff and I agreed that was where we wanted to be all the time. God was working! I could see God working, it was amazing! Geoff told his new boss we were moving out of Illinois in January and could start work the middle of January. Back in the Chicago area we got ready for the big move.

The Christmas season was upon us and so was the snap of cold winter weather. My Volunteer Counselors were anxious about a new Center Director. I told them honestly I didn't know about the progress. A few were very upset.

Whenever I enquired I was told, "Not yet." So I kept doing my job and prayed that God would still have a smile on His face about the job I was doing.

We got our finances in order and set an appointment for a rental truck. We were waiting for January. My good friend from work, Patti, had left the Center, but we kept in contact. Patti was my sounding board. She could see what the leadership was putting me through. She got married in November 2004 and was very happy to find her Prince Charming. And that he was! She'd been through some very tough times. It was bittersweet for me, knowing I was leaving my good friend and her new hubby, Mark. We all had our own journeys that God put us on. We knew we would stay in touch.

The weeks of December arrived and I wound down my job at the Center. I told Grace in November, that I would like to a have a party for my Volunteers Counselors. We were staying with Grace and I felt the need to get her permission. She thought it was a great idea. Grace loved entertaining in her home and was happy to host the party. We decided on a week before Christmas. We understood the busy schedule everyone had, but we prayed God would bring them to the Christmas Party.

Some of my Volunteers Counselors continued to ask about the Center Director search. I had to tell them there was still nothing to report. I realized that they didn't want me to train the new Director. One day my boss said, "Pati, I'm faxing over some papers for you to sign. It's for your exit interview. Be honest," she said. "Be very honest and up front."

I filled out the papers, but needed more space to express myself. I collected my thoughts on what and how to say it in a way that would please God. "The years at the Center were mixed, but I knew God brought me here to help other women in crisis, and He knew I could receive the healing I needed from my three abortions. I so much wanted the Center to do other things for the clients—not just give them stuff—to give a hand up, not a hand out. I knew that there were other programs out there in the communities to help our clients in other ways, but I wanted to help our clients with programs pertaining to taking care of a baby.

"It has been frustrating how it was all received. I admit I was weak in some areas, but I knew some of my weaknesses would turn into strengths. I just want to be remembered at the Center as someone who loved Jesus Christ—and had a heart for the unborn and the women and men suffering from abortions."

I sat back, re-read what I typed and knew it was the truth from my heart. I was happy with what I wrote. I faxed it to my boss, and then called and told her I had done what she wanted. "I have just one question," I said. "On the top of the page it was titled, 'Exit Interview Part One.' What does it mean?" She told me the "Second Part" was the actual exit interview, and that we would talk about what I wrote. I agreed, "Okay, no problem." We set a date for Thursday, December 30th at 10:00 a.m.

I started to pack up my office of personal things I had collected in the four years I was associated with the Center. Memories popped out from different corners of the Center. One day after the Center was closed, I walked into each room and cried as I recalled the lives that were changed there.

Decisions were made there—good and bad. Tears were shed. Hearts were broken and torn apart. I remembered the good things—babies that came in the doors with their moms—the smiles and coos when we were privileged to hold the babies. The women that were healed from their abortions—I remembered the faces—Black, White, Latino, and Chinese. Women of all faiths walked though these doors.

Then there was the basement we totally changed to help the Counselors Volunteers to serve our clients better. There were days when I talked with between five and nine girls about my abortions, praying they would hear my heart and choose life for their babies.

Some days it felt all I was doing was weeping and praying for these clients. I asked God to get me out of this place, because it was too painful to keep telling women what I had done with three of my children. God in His wisdom and love allowed me to see a little bit of His heart. God showed me that my heartache was not in vain.

One day a girl came into the Center. She was very late for her appointment. We were getting ready to close when she appeared on the doorstep. She saw Sheila getting ready to put the "CLOSED" sign up and asked if she could still come in for her appointment. She needed diapers for her little girl—and needed to talk.

Sheila asked me what to do. I said, "Yes, let her in." I sat in my office finishing up last minute paperwork. About 10 minutes later, Sheila entered my office and asked if I could come into the counseling room to talk with her client who was talking about an abortion she had a while back. Sheila thought I was the perfect one to talk with her.

So I dropped everything—like I always did when it came to a client's problem of this nature. The client, Tina, had a little baby girl about seven months old. She was able to sit on her own. I was so taken with this beautiful child I asked Tina if I could hold her little girl. I never asked this before when talking with a client, but for some strange reason, I did this time. I noticed how the child in my arms was just beaming. At first I thought, oh, how cute! I had no idea what would happen next. As I talked, the client reached over, grabbed my arm and twisted it.

Then Tina said, "Miss Pati, don't you remember me at all?"

"I am really embarrassed," I said. "I'm so sorry that I don't. We see so many clients a month—sometimes I forget faces. I am so sorry!"

"Miss Pati," she said, "my boyfriend and I were in your office more than a year ago. You were our counselor. You told us about your three abortions and how your life went downhill from there. You told us about all the drugs, drinking—and just how your family ended up." With tears in her eyes, she continued, "Miss Pati, you are holding my abortion in your arms!"

My heart couldn't contain what I heard. My jaw dropped, tears welled in my eyes, and one by one they slid down my face and onto my clothes. I realized the precious soul I held in my arms, smiling at me, was alive because I told her mom about my three abortions. I was overwhelmed with emotion. I saw Tina and my counselor, Sheila, crying. I looked at the little one I held in my arms. She had fallen asleep with a little smile on her face, as if to say, "Thank you, Miss Pati. You saved my life."

As I gazed at this little girl, my heart ached for my three babies. Before Tina left, we prayed with her. We supplied the diapers she needed and told her about our Post-Abortion Recovery Program. I said that it would be good for her to go through. We knew it would help her with her past abortion. We told her to come back to see us. I told her I would love to see her and her beautiful daughter again. But as God would have it that was the very last time I would see this precious little soul.

XII

WHAT A ROLLER COASTER RIDE

The day of the party I was throwing for my Volunteers Counselors arrived. I looked forward to seeing all of them. The guests, including former volunteers and staff, arrived at Grace's house. I was happy that they took time to come and say goodbye one week before Christmas. At one point I went into the bathroom to collect myself because I was so overwhelmed with emotion. Grace got everyone together and I was presented with a beautiful wrought iron stand with baskets and shelves for coffee, tea and sugar. Everyone agreed it would look great in my Florida kitchen.

I had a gift for Grace—Sue, a client had come to the Center with her boyfriend Evan, almost three years before. I asked Sue to come later so Grace wouldn't see her right away. Grace was her Volunteer Counselor. Grace, Carol and I talked with the couple. They decided to keep their baby and came to visit us at the Center. It was Sue and Evan that Grace and I couldn't get out of my office fast enough when they visited the Center with their precious little one. I invited Sue and her daughter, two-year old Katy. I told Grace to sit down and close her eyes. We motioned for Sue and little Katy to come into the room. When she opened her eyes, they were standing right in front of her. Grace broke down and cried, hugged Sue and little Katy.

Grace told everyone at the party—with Sue's permission—about what happened. But the Belle of the Ball was little Katy! They stayed for a while, then had to leave because Katy needed a nap. It was a very emotional time for me, saying goodbye to these precious women of God who cared so much for the women and the unborn. After everyone left, Grace left for a family party, so I was by myself. I was very tired and sat in the dining room, which looked out over her porch and swimming pool and a beautiful lake. The sun was dipping into the winter sky and I saw the cold winds blowing a bit of snow over the lake. I sat and read the cards and notes. One card stood out. My Volunteer Counselor Barbara wrote, "I've been touched by an angel and I will never forget you, ever. You have changed my life and I thank you for it."

I thanked God for allowing me to be a part of her life and all the other women's lives. I thanked God for the almost 40 volunteers at Grace's house that day. They meant so much to me.

As the day of the exit interview approached, I was busy making sure the Center was in tiptop shape for the new Center Director. On the day of my exit interview my boss showed up around 9:45 a.m. We talked for a bit and then I was told they had just hired someone to be the new Center Director. I was very pleased. I said, "Why did you wait so long to hire a new Center Director?"

"With the old Center getting a face=lift, they just didn't have time to look for one," she explained. I sensed something was wrong, but couldn't put my finger on it.

My boss handed me six pages to read and sign. I read the first page and had the wind knocked out of me. They ripped me up one side and down the other. I read the lies written about me. Then I stopped. "Why are you doing this to me?"

"You didn't do what you were told to do regarding to the Center's hours and what the higher management of the Center said to do. Then when you did, you questioned the reasons." I was accused of not following company procedures and being insubordinate. She told me, "You had Volunteer Counselors that did not go through training prior to counseling. They were in the rooms, counseling."

"We spoke about this," I reminded her. "The new volunteers were never in the room alone. There was always an experienced seasoned Volunteer Counselor—and they never said anything, they just sat and listened. But they did go through training, when you made it available. Or did you forget that!"

"You were always asking for help—staff wise. You complained that you only got help once in awhile," she answered.

I took a deep breath. "If I didn't need another staff person to help, I would not have asked for it. You knew that this Center was just as busy as yours!" I shook my head.

"You know God sees what you are doing. You should be ashamed of yourself!"

"You have tunnel vision and were very negative with Volunteer Counselors and clients," she accused. "Some of the staff complained about you, and so did your Volunteer Counselors."

I knew I had a good relationship with my Volunteer Counselors so I said, "You know, it's funny—if my Volunteer Counselors were complaining about me, why do you think they all attended a party this weekend, gave up their holiday time and gave me a wonderful gift?" "And who was the staff complaining about me?"

She had no response to my questions and changed the subject. "About six or seven months ago I was going to fire you," she said.

I couldn't believe what I was hearing. "Why didn't you fire me?"

"I couldn't. I was being disobedient to God."

"I don't understand what you are saying to me," I said.

"God told me to fire you," she said.

I knew God saw what was going on and I needed to remain calm. The more she talked the more upset I became. She had negative documentation as far back as 2003. I asked, "If I was so bad, why didn't you get rid of me then? And when I told you and the other boss I was leaving, why did she tell me I had done a great job for the past four years? Was that just words?" There was silence.

As I continued to read the exit interview I was expected to sign, I saw a date of May 18. "What is this date about?" I asked.

"Our boss came by to see you and the Center was closed. She saw you with two Volunteer Counselors doing nothing." I reached over and pulled out a file of schedules. I found May 18. I pointed it out to her and asked her to read it. She said, "Well maybe she got the dates wrong."

"You see, I was in Louisville, Kentucky that weekend, because it was the third birthday of my granddaughter, Emily. If you are going to accuse someone, maybe you'd better have your facts correct. And no one can see into the Center. It is not on street level. And when we are closed, the window shades are down. She could not possibly see anyone in the Center. We were closed because I was not there." I couldn't believe this was happening. I felt as if I was talking to people I had never met. Just a few weeks before, they were so nice and pleasant at our staff Christmas party. This was a huge slap in my face!

"You need to sign the papers," she insisted.

"I am not signing anything!" I slammed the papers down on the desk.

"Well, that is your right, but you should sign it anyway— and write underneath that you don't agree with anything." I knew better than to sign those papers. I wondered how stupid she thought I was. I would not get tangled up in all this mess. It seemed they ripped apart everything I did for the last year of the four years I worked there. "Pati," she said, "all your Volunteer Counselors will need to be trained all over again because of the negativity you gave them." Just then a couple of my Volunteer Counselors knocked on my door. They wanted to put their coats away in the closet.

Smiling, I said, "Come in." I didn't want them to see what was happening.

After they left and closed the door, she picked up where we left off. "If you are not going to sign these papers, we are done here."

"May I work Saturday, January 1? I want to get last minute paperwork done and leave the Center in good condition for the new Director.

She smiled. "Yes, you could do that."

She prepared to leave. "You know," I said, "I can't believe you're treating me like this. You should be ashamed, treating a sister in Christ this way."

"Goodbye," she said quietly. She left my office and the building.

So here I was, trying to put a big smile on my face for my Volunteer Counselors. I knew these were my last days with these precious ladies and I would let nothing get in the way of this. But my heart had received a crushing blow. Geoff dropped by on his way to see our Pastor. He came into the Center as my boss was leaving and saw the look on my face. I took him into my office and closed the door. I told him what happened.

Geoff was not surprised. "Honey, look at the way they've been treating you these past years," he said quietly. I knew he was right, but wanted to believe the best of people. After he left I had a very sweet time with my Volunteer Counselors. The Center closed and all my goodbyes were said. I called my friend Cindy—our Pastor's wife—and asked if she would be home—I needed to talk to someone. I got into my car and took a deep breath. I hadn't eaten, so I picked up a burger. All the brain twisting and heart tugging finally got the best of me. As fast as lighting, the tears came. The pain was so deep, intense and raw. At one point I couldn't see the road or catch my breath. I kept praying. "God, why did this happen? Did I do something wrong? Help me, please. Did I not serve You well?" A few seconds later the radio station I was listening to—Moody Radio—played a song by Mark Shultz. It was about being wounded in battle. I knew God heard my cries for help. That song brought me so much peace in my heart. I felt God comforting me.

When I got to Cindy's house I showed her the papers my boss wanted me to sign. "Are you kidding me?" she asked in disbelief.

"I knew things were not the greatest with my boss, but I didn't think they wanted to fire me!" I said. Cindy told me it was good that Geoff and I were moving to Florida— it would be a brand new start for us. Later when Geoff and Pastor C arrived, the four of us prayed together. We asked God to comfort me and take care of the Center, the clients and the staff still there. Pastor C was really upset the way I was treated, but agreed with his wife it was time for a new beginning. We said goodbye and thanked them for helping with the Center and for being such good friends.

The next day I woke up more tired than usual. I believe it was all the stress. When I got downstairs, Geoff was already having coffee. Grace was getting ready for her day. As I walked down stairs, I told myself to get my act together. I heard my phone ringing and saw the Center had left a message. My body started to tense up. What did they want—to hit me again?

Geoff asked, "Now what?" I told them the Center called.

Then Grace chimed in. "Why don't they just leave you alone?" I shook my head, took a deep breath and called back.

The receptionist, Sandy, answered the phone. I told her someone had called me but did not leave a message. She said, "Oh yeah, hold on."

While I waited, I prayed. "Dear God, now what do they want from me? Help me! Didn't they do enough damage yesterday?"

When my boss got on the phone, her voice was very raspy. "Pati, today is your last day and I don't want to argue about it."

"Why? You told me there was no problem with me working on Saturday, so I could get my last minute paper work done. You even thought it was a good idea. What happened?"

"No," she snapped. "Today is your last day—period!"

"Then why did you tell me there was no problem? If you didn't want me to work, why didn't you tell me yesterday?"

"I thought about it last night," she said, "and changed my mind." I knew something was up. She must have spoken with higher up management. Then I realized—of course— they didn't want to pay me for January. That would put me into a new year and able to claim my vacation weeks! I hadn't even thought of that. I just wanted to make sure the Center was okay and paperwork in order.

I threw my cell phone across the room. Why did I even care? Then I ran into the living room and plopped into a chair, breathing hard. Geoff tried to calm me down.

I heard Grace in the other room. "This is just sick—so sick. These can't be Christian women. How can they treat anybody like this?" She came into the living room. "Pati, you were a good Center Director and a friend to everyone at the Center. Your bosses are just jealous of the relationships you've built while you were there. These people don't have half the heart you did for those clients." She gave me a long hug.

Geoff hugged me and held me in his arms. My spirit was broken. I stained his shirt with my tears. "You know," I said trying to calm down. "I used to work with people a long time ago that didn't even believe in Jesus Christ—and they treated me much better than this!"

"This is just so sick," Grace repeated angrily.

When Bob came home and saw what was going on, he was as upset as the rest of us. He mumbled under his breath, "How could these women do such a thing?" Grace agreed with him. I could see the love of Christ in both of them. I felt so blessed to have them in my life. God knew I was going to need it.

On New Year's Eve day the Center was closed. I did my best to take care of the office and paperwork for the new Director. I was alone. I called my friend Patti, and asked if she would meet me at the Center. I knew she heard the tone of my voice. She agreed and said, "I'll be there."

Around 11:00 a.m. I began to go through paperwork. I took a few pictures down from the walls that some of my

Volunteer Counselors gave me. I sat back in my chair and smiled, remembering all the great moments I had with them. As I started down Memory Lane, I saw Patti's car pull into the parking lot. I met her at the back door and burst into tears. She gave me a hug. "Come on, Girlie, let's talk."

We went into my office. "You know, they really don't have a clue anymore. I don't even know if they have the heart they used to." Patti no longer worked at the Center. She'd been gone for several months. She totally understood what I was talking about. But then we started to talk about the good times we had when we did work together—all the tears and laughter—all the clients we helped. We remembered the crazy phone calls— and the client who wanted to take a full crib on the bus. Oh that poor man!

We laughed about our two Bubbas—her husband, Mark and my cat. Both had hearing problems. We talked a little while longer, carried away on the memories of the babies that were saved, and women whose lives we touched— women hearing the Gospel and many trusting Jesus Christ as their Savior. We said, "Goodbye," and hoped to see each other again. I thanked her for being there for me, being a good listener and a great friend.

The night crawled across the Midwest sky, and it was cold. I sat in my office and saw a light streaming from the receptionist's window. I went out to see the most beautiful sunset ever. I pulled up a chair, sat and gazed at the sky. I thanked God for my eyes to see such beauty. I knew it would be the last sunset I would see from the Center. God put on a fabulous show for me that night. It was as if He were telling me, "Well done, my good and faithful servant."

After the sun went down and the sky turned dark, I went back into my office to finish a few things. I boxed up some personal items and brought them to my car. Around 9:30 p.m. I faxed my last time sheet, sat back in my chair and checked the office for the last time. I saw the two wing back chairs in my office and thought of all the clients who sat and made the decision—life or abortion.

I walked into each room that night, sat down, prayed—and thanked God for using me in a powerful and mighty way. I knew it was only through Christ that I was able to do any of this. I knew if I did anything without Jesus Christ, I would surely have failed. I went around and made sure everything was in order, neat and clean. I walked back into my office, picked up my purse, and turned out the lights for the last time. I felt God walking with me that night.

As I locked the back door, a little pot of dirt caught my eye. It was one of the old pots I used to plant spring and summer flowers. I looked at the old pot with dirt and knew God brings life back. My life would be in full bloom again. I put one foot into the pot and then the other. I actually and symbolically—shook off the dirt off my feet and never looked back.

A few days later, some of my Volunteer Counselors wanted to get together with me for a last lunch. We had a great time laughing and crying about all the things we went through together.

As I was about to leave, I called Geoff to let him know I was on my way and it may take some time to get home. It had just begun to snow and I knew he would be concerned. He sounded upset and I asked him what was wrong. "We'll talk when you get home," he said. Then he said, "I just got off the phone with the lady that does your paycheck. She told me you couldn't go in to get your check—that it was going to be mailed to you.

"I told the woman on the phone that, for the past four years you'd always gone to the Center to pick up your check. I asked her what was going on. She said she was told to mail it."

"I said, 'Okay, why don't you give me the name of the person who told you to mail it and I'll call her to see what's going on.'

"The woman said, 'I don't have the number.'

"Then I asked her, 'Why are you treating Pati like this?" Isn't she supposed to get her check on Friday?'

"She said, 'Yes.'"

Then Geoff said to the woman, "You also told me that if you mail it, she would get it by Friday.

"The woman said 'Yes.'

"So I said, 'It's Wednesday, late afternoon. Did you mail the check yet?'

"She said, 'No.'"

Geoff asked, "Then if we don't get it by Friday, which is Pati's payday, what are you prepared to do?"

He told me there was dead silence on the phone, and then he heard her say, "If I give it to Pati, it's my butt!"

Geoff asked her again, "So what are you prepared to do?"

There was silence on the phone. Then he heard her say, very quietly, "You can come pick it up." Geoff thanked her and asked her what time would be good and she said, "Nine a.m."

Geoff was sorry he told me right then, because he knew I was having a great time with my Volunteer Counselors. I said goodbye to Geoff and told him I'd be careful driving home.

My Volunteer Counselors saw I was an emotional wreck. "Pati, what's wrong?" they asked. I didn't want to tell them, but I couldn't hold it in. None of us could understand why management would do such a thing. I changed the subject. We talked for a few more minutes. I hugged each one of them.

One of my Volunteers Counselors, Flo, and I had some great talks, and she prayed with me often. She loved Jesus Christ and being at the Center. She told me she would miss me so much. I told each of them how much I loved them and what an honor and joy it was to work with Godly women preaching the good news about Jesus Christ. I knew how much they loved helping women make the choice for life. We got in our cars and headed for home.

On my drive home I made sure to pay attention to the roads because it was snowing hard. I thought about what I was going to do next, about the phone call with Geoff and why this was happening. I felt as if I was drowning. Every time I came up for air, I was pushed down again. I heard great music on the radio, which brought my stress level down. When I arrived at Grace's house, I was pretty calm. I told Geoff, I'd go to the Center with him to get my paycheck. I agreed to stay in the car. He told me he didn't want me near them.

Friday arrived and so did we at the Center. Usually we'd go to the back of the Center to get our checks. This day, they were waiting up front. Geoff told me what happened. My boss sat with her arms folded, and the woman with the check sat beside her. As soon as he approached the door, she jumped up and handed him the check. He noticed she was shaking. Geoff stood there and made sure they paid me what was owed me. The receptionist told Geoff to have a safe trip. He didn't respond, knowing he wouldn't be able to say anything nice. He walked out the door.

When Geoff got in the car, I was on my cell phone talking with Flo. She called to tell me how badly she felt. She told me to forget about what happened. She was so sorry I had to go through all of this. She had no idea what was going on. I thanked her for loving, kind words and her friendship. I told her I'd miss her! She prayed for me while she was still on the phone. I felt very blessed.

Geoff told me that my boss and everyone, looked like the Gestapo. I checked my paycheck to see if everything was in order. There was a letter attached to it. "Pati's check should have included three weeks paid vacation and five sick days."

This upset me. "Look here," I said to Geoff, "even the computer realizes that I should be getting paid vacation time. They just crossed it out."

Geoff pulled out of the Center parking lot. He saw his wife of 31 years—–broken, beat up, knocked down and dragged all over the place. The faster I wiped my tears, the more I cried. He reached over to hold my hand, "Pati, just let it go, Honey. It's all done."

"How can I just let go of four years of my life just like that?" I felt so empty, like someone had torn my heart out and thrown it away. I looked out my car window and felt as cold as the Midwest sky. As we drove, God brought memories of those babies that came in with their moms, the looks on the mothers' faces—and the sparkle in their eyes. I heard them saying, "Thank you for being here and telling me about your hurts and shames—because if it wasn't for you, our children wouldn't be here now. And thank you for telling us about Jesus Christ." The reflections of trees and the countryside turned into faces of all the clients and babies I saw. God was smiling on me.

As I thought what God was laying on my heart, I also thought of my children— all five of them. My two sons that were here with us—and what blessings they were to us. Then I thought about our three children in Heaven. What would their lives have been like? What would they have become? What kind of jobs would they have had? How many more grandkids would we have had? As soon as those thoughts entered my mind, God graced me with peace. I settled down in the car and relaxed. It was over.

The last week we lived in the Chicago area, we were invited to so many houses for dinner. Our friends and former neighbors on Campbell Avenue, Deborah and Kerry, had us over for dinner. When we pulled up in their driveway, it felt very different. More friends joined us for dinner. Gina came with her kids. We sat around the table laughing—and crying about all the nutty things we used to do together.

Well, it was time to say goodbye again. I cried and told everyone how much they would be missed. The hardest goodbyes were to Grace and Bob. They left for a vacation in Florida a few days before us. Every time Grace and I looked at each other, we cried. We were so grateful for Grace and Bob and what they did for us. They showed us what Christian love was all about. It's about helping people and loving each other—just as Jesus Christ did.

XIII

LITTLE HANDS ON THE FRONT PORCH

We woke up to an empty house. Grace and Bob had left for Florida—and here was our big day. Geoff and Pastor C picked up the truck, and some friends from the church came to help. It was a cold day. It rained the night before, so the ground was still a little damp. As they loaded the last of our stuff onto the truck, I was amazed how God worked in our lives.

I stood there holding my entire memories close. Then—crash! The back door of the truck closed. We prayed with everyone, said goodbye and were on our way to Florida. I drove Geoff's truck and he drove the rental truck with my car on a trailer. I regretted leaving Geoff Jr.'s two boys behind. They came over to Grace and Bob's house a couple days before we left.

Both boys started to cry. I kept hugging and crying and didn't want to let go. This was so hard to do. They were two sweet little boys. I was sad to leave them behind, knowing I'd not be able to watch them grow up. They really loved their Grandpa! I remembered all the wonderful times we had with them—playing on the staircase with their matchbox cars and then rolling them down the stairs and giggling the whole time. I loved their laughter. We told them they could come visit with Grandpa and Grandma anytime! I knew God would help us all through this.

I was ready for a new beginning! When we got up that morning, the weather wasn't looking too good. As we left Illinois, the clouds over us parted and we were blessed with beautiful rays of sunshine.

We planned to stay with Michael and Beth in Louisville, Kentucky for one night before heading to Florida. The drive to Louisville felt different this time. It wasn't the usual birthday, anniversary and holiday trip. Knowing it would be some time before I was able to see my kids and grandkids caused me deep pain. I secretly asked God if Michael, Beth and the kids could move to Florida. I also asked God if my other grandkids could move to Florida as well. We left two grandkids in Chicago and one granddaughter in Michigan, but I knew God would take care of them.

We arrived in Louisville around 4:00 p.m. and Michael told us to park the truck and trailer at the Southern Seminary parking lot. He met and drove us to his house. Our two little cuties, Emily and Will, waited for us on the front porch— jumping up and down. I jumped up and down inside when I saw them. As Michael parked we heard, "Grandma and Grandpa are here!" That night we had a great time. Beth cooked a wonderful dinner. If the children misbehaved there was a special corner where they had to stand. I was amazed how they wouldn't move unless Michael or Beth pardoned them. Emily loved to dress up like a fairy princess. She had two outfits—one Snow White and the other, Cinderella. She accessorized her little gowns with necklaces, rings and her princess shoes—sometimes on the wrong foot. She twirled around, "Look at me Grandma, I am a fairy princess!" I picked her up, twirled her around and put her down. She twirled away.

I did the same thing in front of my grandmother when I was young. I prayed Emily wouldn't do some of the same things I did. As I thought about that I got tears in my eyes. Emily saw the tears, came over and hugged me, smiled at me and twirled away.

William, on the other hand, loved his Grandpa Geoff. William always carried small matchbox racecars with him. Grandpa got on the floor with him and played racecars. As he got older, the floor didn't work for him, so it was off to the races on a couch or chair. Grandpa Geoff told William he had old knees. William stood looking at Grandpa's knees, with a quizzical look on his face. It was pretty funny!

Abby was five months old, but she stole our hearts with her huge blue eyes. She sat on our laps and was so cute! She had the habit of scrunching up her nose before she smiled. I was amazed at how fast our grandchildren were growing. When the kids where ready for bed Michael and Beth held devotional time. Michael read a story from the Children's Bible. Usually both kids listened, but now and then William rolled around on his bed—just being a three year old. Michael stopped reading and told him to sit still.

He told his son this was God's time. Michael looked at me and I giggled. I couldn't help noticing how cute he was. Then I'd give William the "Grandma eye" to sit still. Other times he'd make funny faces or flip over so he was sitting on his head.

I'd put my hand in front of my mouth. It was hard not to laugh, but if he saw that—oh boy, William and I would be in trouble with Michael! Ever so often Emily would scold, "Stop Willie!" After devotions, Emily and William recited a verse from the Old Testament. Geoff and I were impressed how fast they were learning.

The next morning Beth made a huge breakfast. I knew in my heart we had to leave, but tried not to think about it. I wanted to enjoy my family. About an hour after breakfast, Geoff signaled me, silently telling me he wanted to get on the road.

Beth packed us snacks, bottled water and goodies for the trip. I had done it so many times, I no longer knew how to say goodbye. Then Emily climbed in my lap, hugged me and wouldn't let go. She hung onto me, whispering something I couldn't hear. I asked her, "Emily, honey, what's the matter? What are you saying?"

Emily answered, in her small voice. "Grandma, I want you to stay here so I can see you tomorrow. I am very sad you're going away." Oh that child just broke my heart! I knew it was going to be hard, but this was too much. I held that precious little one close to me and hugged her with all I had. Emily's tiny arms were wrapped around my neck. She didn't want to let go. She kissed and hugged me, then stood there with those gorgeous blue eyes and told me how much she loved me. I told her how much I loved her and promised we'd see each other soon.

I was still crying when William came to me and wrapped his little arms around me. He hugged me and told me he loved me, too. Then he ran to Geoff. I could see how much he loved his Grandpa who was having a hard time letting go of his grandson. William wrapped his arms around his Grandpa, and would not let go.

We showered Abby with tons of kisses. I walked over to Michael, hugged and kissed him and told him how proud I was of him. I thanked God he'd grown up to be a wonderful husband and father. Michael said, "Mom, I'll miss you. You've done your job raising kids and now it's time for you and Dad." I guess I needed to hear that from my son.

I turned around to Beth. She was already crying. To me, she was my daughter. I watched how she and Michael were with the kids, how they loved them and disciplined them when they needed it. But the best part was seeing how she loved Michael! It was easy to see how much they loved each other. I stood there for a moment and thought how much I wanted a happy home for my sons and their families.

Geoff gently nudged me. It was time to go. Michael walked us to our truck. Beth and the kids stayed on the front porch. The picture of those tiny little hands on the front porch, waving goodbye is burned into my memory.

XIV

CLOUDS IN FLORIDA

It rained when we left Louisville—and it continued all the way to Georgia. We wanted to make it to Macon, Georgia by 7:00 p.m., but it was dark and pouring down rain. I called Geoff on his cell. "I need to stop, I can't drive anymore."

We found a hotel outside Atlanta and rested for the night. The next morning the weather was much nicer. As we entered Florida, my mind was filled with anticipation about my new life there. What kind of job would I have? Where would we live? We were to stay with friends of ours, Allan and Maria, for a week or two. The last time we lived in Jacksonville, I helped Maria learn to drive. We had fun together. We loved going to garage and tag sales on Saturday mornings. She always found great buys—and it always amazed me.

Pastor Carr called and wanted to know when we were moving back to Jacksonville. I told him we just arrived. He said, "Well then, I guess I'm your welcoming committee. Welcome back!"

Someone from the church must have told him we were moving back. He is a great guy. He was the High School Pastor and took care of the High School Ministry. We met him when our son Michael was involved with high school programs at the church. Pastor Carr had a huge heart for these high school kids, and helped Michael so much in his walk with the Lord. Michael enjoyed being around him. Pastor Carr always had time to talk with us. He said how much he loved helping Michael and how he could see our son growing in his faith. It was nice for him to be the first person we talked to when we got back to Jacksonville. He asked if I was going to come back to work at the church. I told him I wasn't sure. I was waiting to see what doors God opened for me.

I applied at the church for a secretarial position, but my heart wasn't in it. It was at the Crisis Pregnancy Center. As I prayed one day, I remembered telling my Volunteer Counselors if I couldn't get a job working a Center, I would volunteer. Oh yeah, Volunteer! I remembered there was a Center in Jacksonville. One day I walked in and asked to speak with the Executive Director. We talked for a while. I told her what I did in the Chicago area, working at a Crisis Pregnancy Center. She told me they were just about to open a Center at the beach and were looking for staff help. Then she said it was not going to be until March. My heart sank. It was only January, and I really needed a job right away.

I filled out the application and mailed it. One of the questions on the application was if they could contact my last employer. I sat there for a while. I was not sure what to say. I asked my boss before I left Chicago if they would give me a good report for a new job. She said, "By law, we can only say when you worked here and for how long. We can say you were a Center Director—and that is it!"

I knew the Center where I was applying would want to hear more about my role and volunteers and so on. I knew if I was interviewing a person and that was all I got, I'd be inclined not to hire that person. I wasn't sure what would be said about me. The best thing I could do was trust God. I heard a little voice in the back of my mind saying the only way I would get this job was to lie. I didn't lie—I told the truth.

Every time I applied for jobs in the past I would be hired within three days or so. While I waited, Geoff and I went riding on the Harley. We always had a great time together doing that. As I was riding, I was praying that I would hear from them really soon.

March finally arrived. I called the Center and was told they weren't interviewing until the end of March. When I got off the phone, I thought maybe I needed to look elsewhere. I knew God was getting ready to do something. My not working was putting a load on Geoff. He took a huge pay cut leaving Chicago to go to Jacksonville. It seemed like my life was on hold. Some days I felt God walking right along with me. On other days I felt abandoned. While in this waiting period, I learned that Michael was getting ready to go on a mission trip to India.

I was concerned about him leaving Beth and the three kids, but a phone call from Beth changed my heart. She told me Michael was giving his testimony at their church. He shared about fighting with his brother, the big accident Geoff Jr. had, and his brother being so far away from God. He also shared that something happened to Geoff Jr. a year before, and he started to read the Bible and attend church services. Michael said he could see a change in his brother's life.

Beth told me Michael was actually having conversations with his brother about God and the Bible. He never dreamed that would happen, and tears of joy flooded his face. She also said Michael showed people in their church an arrow given to him by a man in a tribe overseas who told Michael that he and his family had no hope. Children were sacrificed to their gods. There was a lot of pain and death. Michael told him the good news of Jesus Christ and the hope of eternal salvation. The man was so moved, he gave Michael an arrow as a constant reminder to come back with more missionaries, so his people could hear this wonderful news and find joy.

As he shared this with the congregation, Beth said Michael was so moved he stood there with tears streaming down his face. "You could have heard a pin drop."

At that moment Emily stood up in the pew and in a loud voice said, "Daddy you've got to go and tell people about Jesus!" Then she sat down. All that could be heard were people crying and blowing their noses.

After I heard that, all the worries of Michael going on the mission ended. My family was changing all around me, and it was good. So what was God up to? One morning while I had my Bible and quiet time, I read Haggai Chapter 1: 3-6.

"Is it then the right time for you to live in luxurious homes, when the temple lies in ruins? Look at the result: you plant much but harvest little. You have scarcely enough to eat or drink, and not enough clothes to keep you warm. Your income disappears, as though you were putting it into pockets filled with holes!"

When I read that I sat and cried. Was this what my life was about—trying to get the big house, big stuff? After I saw what was going on with the Center I just left in Chicago—after all the girls and women in crisis—and the unborn babies being slaughtered. The women and men whose lives were radically changed from past abortions—who was going to help them? What did it matter about this material junk, when God's people were crying out for help? I couldn't stop crying, as I thought of all those women and men hurting! I asked myself why I felt so pulled to help? Why did God want to use me? Could He use someone else? I did not want to read something into the scripture or take it out of context about my situation now, but I was so taken back by what I read. I put my head on the Bible and felt God was touching my heart! What a great day!! Guess what, I did not cry!!

XV

SECRETLY ACHING

During my time of waiting for a job, I tried to spend more time reading the Bible. After doing so, I remembered the dreams I had, and one popped up several times. It was when I counseled the women and girls before the pregnancy test was given. I found out a little bit about them and their thoughts on the possibility of being pregnant. As I watched, legs shook, feet tapped, tears flowed. I saw the nerves pour out of them. They were petrified. Most of the time what I heard was, "If I am pregnant, I will have nowhere to go." "My mom will kick me out of the house." I did hear those words a lot. There were a few girls whose moms did let them keep their babies. But other girls really did not have a place to go. There were only two maternity homes that we knew about, but with the number of girls we had, we needed 50 or more maternity homes!

My heart broke for these women and girls. Each day as I drove to work, I passed by so many empty hotels, most of them had three or more floors. I thought what a great place any of them would be to have a maternity home. They usually had one entrance, each room had its own bathroom. Easily two girls could share each room. Every floor could be monitored. We could provide parenting, Bible and computer classes, as well as assistance in attaining GEDs. We could help in how to write a resume, balance a checkbook, dress for an interview and apply makeup. We could even provide etiquette classes. We could share with them all things needed to care for herself and her baby. Should the issue arise, we could talk to them about adoption. If these girls where given half the chance, there would be less moms and dads suffering from abortion—and there would be more precious little ones born. Nine times out of ten these women and girls think nobody cares for them. They figure if Mom, Dad, Grandparents and boyfriend don't care, why should anyone else care. Who will be there to pick up the pieces of their abandoned, torn life? Many chose abortion because they felt there was nowhere to go and it was easier to get an abortion and move on with their lives. But that is not the case. This decision will haunt them for the rest of their lives. I know! This is one of the dreams that I thought about almost every day.

It was the last week of March and I finally got the call. I was so excited. I had an interview with Carrie and thought the interview went well. She said she would get back to me. I guess I expected an answer that moment, since I waited so long for this day to come. After a week with no word, I was getting nervous, so I called. "Pati," she said, "we had a lot of people apply for that position. We went with someone else, but I hope you still continue to volunteer with us."

I hung up the phone. I just sat on my couch, felt numb, rejected, wondering if I said something wrong. Should I have said something different? Did the Center in Chicago say something negative about me? I felt God abandoned me. I would no longer be able to work at a Crisis Pregnancy Center. But why? I walked around my house in tears, my heart breaking. I felt I wasn't good enough anymore. I was tired of crying all the time.

I asked myself why I couldn't find a job. When we moved into our little apartment on the River, I wondered what the heck I was going to do. Becky, a friend of mine from church, was selling cosmetics and connected me with the company. Becky and I had some really fun times. She was my Sunday School Teacher and a person I could trust and pray with me. But selling cosmetics again, my heart was not in it anymore.

One day I was shopping and ran into another friend. She was the Executive Director for another Crisis Pregnancy Center and told me there was a Center up north, near the beach, looking for a Director or some staff. I contacted that Center and volunteered there. I told the Center in Jacksonville, I was volunteering at a Center closer to my home. The Executive Director at the Jacksonville Center said, "Pati, this is still your heart and I can see it in your face." She was a great lady and encouraged me a lot. So I left the Center that was so far away and volunteered at the closer one. I was happy to be back at the Center. A few weeks later the Center Director hired me as Client Service

Director. This was a part time, paid position. Geoff and I were happy.

But as life would have it, fuel for my car ate up my paycheck. I really could not afford to go to work. I was putting most of my paycheck into the gas tank. I had to find a full time position. My boss at the Center was very understanding. One day a sign caught my attention—a job opening for a Bookkeeper/Head Cashier. I applied, had an interview with the store manager, and got the job working at a Hardware Store!

With all this going on, Michael called to tell us they were moving to Jacksonville to be closer to family. Geoff and I were so excited! They gave us a date for the move. We flew to Louisville and helped them move. Geoff and Michael drove the rental truck. Beth, the kids and I—and Cory the dog, drove in their van.

Geoff Jr. was extremely happy to have his brother living in the same town. I thanked God for another opportunity to have the whole Adams Family together again. Michael's family moved in with us. We were renting a southern long ranch home, with big trees full of hanging moss. We had a fenced=in back yard, which worked out fine for the kids and dog.

A year later, Geoff and I decided to buy a house. We wanted to settle down and stay put. We found a cute little house in the suburbs, with a swimming pool, garage for Geoff and his Harley, and a huge back yard for our grandkids. The day we purchased the home was a really good day. Geoff and I looked at each other and smiled. We finally had a place to call home, settle in and our kids and grandkids—well most of them—were there with us.

I was working at the hardware store. I was unsure about this job for a few months. It was very different from what I had done before. Some of the payroll stuff was not clicking with me. I had to learn the cash register, different items in the store and all the unfamiliar office stuff. I was overwhelmed. I said, "Geoff, I don't think I can do this job."

"Pati," he said, "just take it one day at a time." After awhile it started to click and I began to enjoy my job. I finally found "my groove"

While I worked at the hardware store, I went back to the first Crisis Pregnancy Center in Jacksonville and volunteered every Monday night. It made for long Mondays, but I enjoyed being at the Center where I felt I was helping the women and men in crisis. My co-workers at the hardware store found out I was volunteering at the Crisis Pregnancy Center and were very supportive. They knew the history of my other jobs at the Centers. My office held all the two-way radios for the store. When the warehouse guys picked up theirs, I often heard swearing. I didn't want to hear that stuff in my office.

One day one of the cashiers came into my office with tears in her eyes. "Miss Pati," she whispered, "I need to talk with you."

"Sure. Come in and close the door."

"Do you still volunteer at the Crisis Pregnancy Center?" she asked.

"I sure do. What's up?"

Quietly she said, "I think I'm pregnant." She lowered her head and stared at the floor. I asked her a few questions. "Oh, Miss Pati, What should I do?"

I gave her all the information I could, hugged her and said, "Honey, make sure you talk with your parents."

"I'm afraid I'll ruin the great relationship we have! This might make them think badly about me." She took a deep breath.

"If you were in your parents' shoes, wouldn't you want know what was going on with your daughter?" I asked.

"Yes, I guess so," she agreed, with tears in her eyes. We talked for about 30 minutes.. She thanked me, said she felt much better and we exchanged hugs.

"Please leave the door open when you leave, Dear," I requested. When she was gone, I ran out of my office and stood in the hallway looking at my office door.

The store manager came by. "Are you okay, Pati?" he asked.

I turned my head and said, "Yeah, I think so."

"Why are you staring at your name on the door?"

"You wouldn't understand," I told him.

He walked away laughing. "I guess I wouldn't, Pati. Sometimes you are crazy—just plain crazy!"

Actually, I was checking to see if the nameplate had changed from "Bookkeeper—Pati Adams" to "Crisis Pregnancy Center." I went back into my office, and sat there shaking my head.

Well this scene replayed a few more times with different girls that worked at the store. A couple warehouse guys asked me about condoms and birth control. When I told them what I knew, they were shocked. I also told them, "If you aren't prepared to take care of a baby— stop having sex!" I was very blunt with them. A few of them said they appreciated my being so honest. A couple of them said nobody ever took the time to talk with them about stuff like this. Oh, tests all came up negative for the few girls that thought they were pregnant.

I made some pretty good friends, enjoyed my job and liked the owners of the store. The fact that they were Christian businessmen made the job even more enjoyable. My life seemed to be getting in order. I breathed a huge sigh of relief. Our family loved being with each other for holidays, anniversaries and just coming over to Grandma's and Grandpa's to go swimming. Life was good. But as it stands with me, nothing could stay the same. My life was about to change again!

XVI

NOT READY FOR THIS!

We started our week out as usual—Geoff going to work, me going to work, making plans with our kids for the upcoming weekend. But God had something else in mind for us.

One Monday, when Geoff was at work, he had an accident. He cut himself very deeply and ended up in the Emergency Room needing stitches. Geoff went back to work on Tuesday and all seemed well. When he went to work on Wednesday, he got the bad news that they were laying off one-third of employees—and Geoff was one of them.

I was at Michael and Beth's house when he called me. My first reaction was to pray, "Okay God, You are in control!" I asked Geoff if he wanted to come to Michael and Beth's house.

"I just want to be alone," he said. "I'm going for a drive." He hung up the phone. We got the kids and prayed for Geoff to find comfort in this time of pain. When I got home that night, I found him wondering how we were going to pay the bills, the mortgage and just plain eat.

"Geoff, honey," I reminded him "I'm still working and God will see us through this." I wasn't really sure how, but I was clinging onto Christ.

On Friday when I got home from work, Geoff wanted to take the Harley and go out for pizza, just like we always did on Fridays. "I need some kind of normal in our life," he said, "even if it's just pizza on Friday night." We both liked to ride, so off we went. After we had our pizza dinner, we headed to the drugstore to get some of my medicine. Geoff's insurance was still good for another month.

As we pulled out of the parking lot, I noticed a car coming around the drive. In that split second I knew it was going to hit us. Then I heard Geoff hitting the handlebars on the bike and felt myself fly over him. I landed on my back in the parking lot. The only thing that stopped the car from going any further was our Harley under her car! I heard a lot of commotion. Geoff ran up to me and checked me for broken bones. I told him, "I think I'm okay, but I'm kind of afraid to move." I heard sirens.

The driver that hit us ran over to me, poked me and said, "Honey, Honey are you okay? Are you okay?"

Geoff said angrily, "You already hit her with your car! Stop touching her and poking at her!"

Suddenly there were four EMTs trying to cut my leather jacket off me. "No, please don't," I begged them. "Just take the jacket off!"

They asked me a few questions. "Where do you hurt?" "Can you move your neck?"

They turned me over and another two removed my jacket. They told me they didn't like doing it, but I was pretty insistent.

The police officer told Geoff the driver was listening to loud music in the car—so loud she wouldn't even have heard an ambulance go by her car. She was just not paying attention. "I never saw the motorcycle," she told the police officer.

The officers prepared to get a tow truck for the bike. Geoff said, "No, I'll call a friend of mine." Our friend came with his pickup to get the bike. Then Geoff called our boys. Michael came to help. Geoff Jr. was watching his sleeping daughter, so he couldn't come to help.

When I got to the Emergency Room, I waited for them to do X-rays on me. I closed my eyes and my mind drifted back to another bike accident we had back in 1981....

It was a warm Saturday night and there were about eight of us on bikes. Geoff and I usually rode on Saturday nights, but this was before we started to work at the bar on Saturday nights. One night Geoff pulled into traffic when he accidentally gunned the gas and hit the sand in the driveway. We were pulled into traffic and the bike went down. I flew off the back and landed in the middle of Boston Post Road. Geoff's leg got caught under the bike and he was dragged about 10 feet down the road.

As I lay in the road, cars drove around me. All my girlfriends were screaming to their boyfriends to stop. They pulled their bikes over to the side of the road. The guys ran to Geoff, and the girls ran to me. The bike was lying on top of Geoff. He couldn't get up. They pulled the bike off him. He got up and limped to the side of the road. The girls were waving traffic around me. One of my friends screamed at the top of her lungs, "She is dead! Pati is dead!"

I screamed back at her. "You dimwit! I'm not dead! But I will be if you guys don't get me up, before we all die!" They grabbed me and yanked me up. I hobbled over to Geoff. He was upset because he couldn't get to me. He hugged me and asked if I was okay. I kept telling him, "I'm okay, and I'll be fine. I don't think bones are broken. But you know what? I am very sore. My head, back and butt hurts!"

I was more concerned about Geoff. He took the biggest hit. His leg was badly bruised. His knee was swollen and scraped. His pants were torn from sliding on the road and his jacket was all scraped up. But I thanked God for our leather jackets. They really protected both our skins.

After everyone knew we were okay, they looked at the bike. It had dents and scratches,

but nothing serious. After Geoff got the bike
up and running again, we went back to the
bar and had more drinks—to remove aches
and pains…...

As I thought about this, I saw how stupid we all were.
Just then, one of nurses came in, bringing me back to reality,
to tell me that they were taking me to X-ray to see if I had
any broken bones.

When I returned from the x-ray department I was lying
flat on the backboard in a neck brace. I could see someone
sitting beside me, but couldn't move my neck. My sweet
daughter-in-law Beth reached out and touched my hand.
She moved around the bed so I could see her, and we both
started to cry.

I told her the lady that hit us said she didn't see us. "God
was with you," Beth told me. "Everything is going to be
okay."

Some biker friends visited in the Emergency Room and
prayed with me. Geoff finally made it to the E.R., but
wouldn't let them check him out. Doctors told us we were
very lucky, but the next few days we'd be in really tough
shape with bruising. He also told me I had no broken bones,
but that from my neck to my spine I was riddled with
arthritis.

Michael and Beth took us home around 1:00 a.m. They
walked us into our house, prayed with us and said they
would call later in the day. Weeks later we got a little better.
We spent lots of time sitting on the couch, looking at each
other. "What's next?" we asked.

Geoff was healing, so he went on job interviews with other railroads, but nothing was happening. He was getting pretty discouraged. I kept working and healing—but things were different. We were glad to be near our kids and grandkids, but money was getting really tight. Geoff found the driver that hit us with her brand new two-door, black Mercedes Benz. We found her address and got her phone number. We could see she was wealthy. Geoff called her and said, "We don't plan to sue you, but if you could pay our medical bills and fix the bike—and if you had it in your heart to give us something else—that would be up to you."

She started to cry on the phone and said she couldn't believe that we weren't going to sue her. Geoff told her that we were Born Again Christians and we don't do that. Some of my co-workers told me I was crazy not to sue her. They just couldn't understand my reasoning.

Geoff kept looking for a job, but the searching was turning bleak. A few months later he sent his resume to a railroad in Massachusetts. They called and asked Geoff to come for an interview. I decided to go with him. We flew to Connecticut, rented a car and stayed with my brother Tony in Connecticut. We drove to Massachusetts for the interview. He got the job, but had to start the following month. When we figured out how much it would cost to move, we couldn't figure where we'd get the money. God had the money ready and waiting. It came from the lady who hit us. What she gave us was exactly what we needed to move. Geoff and I were blown away by what God was doing.

We were excited about the money and the job—but we had to move away from our family again—and our home where we thought we could finally settle down. God had other plans for us. Our family was happy for us, but very sad we had to leave them. They helped us pack. The grandkids wanted to know when we could come back to see them again. I told them we didn't know—that with Grandpa's new job, it could be a while.

I couldn't believe we were moving again! We just bought the house, had good jobs, our family was around us—then poof, the rug got pulled out from under us. I knew there was a plan in store for us, but what? A few years earlier, our son Geoff Jr was married again and they had a precious little girl, Natalie. Another wonderful granddaughter, with big brown eyes, and a smile that could melt your heart. And again we had to say good-bye! I called my brother Tony to let him know when we'd arrive. He and my two nephews were there to help us move into the apartment we found in Massachusetts, when Geoff got the job. It was a cute place, but not like our home in Florida. The good thing was not only the job, but I was near my dad, my brothers and their families. We got to Massachusetts a week before Thanksgiving. It was nice spending the holiday with them after so many years. I missed my kids and their families. I told Geoff I wanted to be near my dad in his last years. He had so many health issues when I lived in Florida. I hadn't been able to get up to see him. It was nice to drive only an hour to see him, which we did every week. We spent hours with him and took him grocery shopping. In the spring we took him to get flowers for his patio. He had a very cute little cottage. After a while he couldn't do it any longer, so my brothers and I planted the flowers for him. We put a whole bunch near his sliding glass door so he could see them.

Before we moved I checked for a job at another hardware store up north. When Geoff went to work, so did I— at the hardware store, but I ended up leaving. I knew it was not where God wanted me anymore. My time working at a hardware store was done. I checked at a Crisis Pregnancy Center in Worcester, Massachusetts and met a wonderful lady named Wendy. She was the Client Service Director for the Center. When I told her what I used to do, she was very excited. I told her I would like to volunteer. She said she'd love to have me. I went through their volunteer training, and away I went. Wendy picked my brain for information. She liked knowing how other Centers did things. She thought it might help her Center. We hit it off and felt like we had known each other for years. We had a common ground. We shared the Gospel of Jesus Christ and helped women make a good choice for themselves and their babies. I loved being back in a Center. It was like I was breathing again!

A few months later, it occurred to me I didn't know if there were any Centers in Connecticut—my home state. The Center in Worcester wasn't looking to hire anybody in the near future. Maybe something was in Connecticut. I found a Center that was closer to me than Worcester.

I told Wendy what I was doing. "Pati," she said, "I know that you need a paying job. Let me know what happens." I wasn't sure about leaving Wendy at her Center, but something nagged at me about the Center in Connecticut.

I saw the hours they were open, gathered up my resume and off I went. As I drove, I wondered what I was doing. These people had no clue who I was. Did I think I could just walk up and get a job—just like that? Maybe the cold air was getting to me!

I found the place, walked into the Center and asked to speak to either the Center Director or Executive Director. A few minutes later a very distinguished lady came out and told me her name was Linda. She asked if she could help me. I told her my name, what I used to do, and asked if they needed any help—volunteer or paid staff. She asked me, "Do you have time to talk?"

"Yes," I said, "I sure do!" She took me to one of the counseling rooms. I talked for a bit and then she talked. She asked me a lot of questions. "Pati," she said, taking a deep breath. "I can't believe you're here! For a long time now, I've wanted to retire. I could never find anyone with the experience to replace me." I sat there with my mouth open! She continued. "I need to get your resume to the Board of Directors. Would you be willing to come and speak with them?" I think I still had my mouth open, because she had to repeat it. She asked, "Are you okay?"

I nodded my head and said, "Oh yes! Oh yes! I am okay—except I think I'm in shock!"

"I could have never imaged that someone with your experience as a Center Director would just come walking through that door, looking for a job! I needed someone to take my place, because I want to retire!" She sat back in her chair. We both knew God was all over this.

As we continued our conversation, what just happened kind of overwhelmed us both. "Well it's time for me to get going," I said once it all sank in.

"I'll definitely be in touch," she said as we walked out to the waiting room. I got in my car and sat there, still in disbelief. I laughed at myself as I remembered the conversation I had with myself before I got to the Center. "Yeah, I am just going to walk into the Center and get a job!" Well, that's what it looked like. All I had to do was wait for the phone call from Linda.

When Geoff came home from work, he couldn't believe my story. "You know," he said, "every time we think we're moving because of my job, God puts you into a Crisis Pregnancy Center. I think I am just along for the ride! God seems to be giving you these jobs for a reason. He has called you to this ministry and wants you still in this."

A week later, I received an e-mail from Linda wanting to know if I could meet with the Board of Directors in a few weeks. She said they only met once a month and they'd like to interview me. She gave me the date. I got off the phone wondering how many Board Members there were!

The big day arrived and I was a little nervous—okay, I was a lot nervous—as I drove to the Center, but I knew God was with me and I'd be okay. The Board Members were very nice and easy to talk to. I was confident as I answered the questions, so I felt it was a good interview. They said that they'd been praying to open a new Center in Willimantic.

They asked me to wait downstairs in the Center and said someone would be down to talk with me in 15 or 20 minutes. Linda and I went downstairs, into a counseling room to chat. She thought the interview went really well. The President of the Board, Pastor Mike, came down to talk with me. He couldn't believe I just walked into the Center like this— looking to volunteer or to see if they had a paying position. "We all believe that God definitely had a hand in it." He continued, "We want to offer you the job.

"You will be taking over a little Center we have in Storrs, near the University of Connecticut as Center Director. Linda will train you to take over the job of Executive Director, overseeing the little Center and the Center here in Danielson. She'll be leaving her position the end of May and they will be all yours!" He traded glances with Linda and they smiled.

My heart was so happy. I couldn't believe this was happening. "Does this mean I'm hired?" I asked.

Pastor Mike grinned. "Oh, most definitely you are hired!" We talked a little more about salary and hours, and then he had to leave. I stayed a little while. Linda showed me around the Center and introduced me to some of the volunteers and staff. They wanted me to start the following week. I was ready—ready for a new challenge—ready to see what God was going to do with my life.

I told my friend Wendy in Worcester, and she was excited for me, but sad I was leaving her. I said we could still get together and talk, which we did.

On the first day of my new job I met more volunteers and staff. Linda was putting together two banquets. It was a lot of work, but she pulled it off. I guess 10 years of being an Executive Director will do that. She trained me and told me she wanted me to start praying about a Center in Willimantic area. The Board wanted to put a Center there for years. "But," she said, "This is your baby now. You do what you need to do."

While I was at the Center I met a wonderful woman named Lynn that was volunteering at the Danielson Center. She lived in Willimantic, so she knew all the areas of town. I asked Linda if I could pick up the ball and start looking. "Go for it!" she said. I did.

I met with Lynn. She found us a few places. The first one we checked out was right on Main Street. She called the landlord, Jerry and asked if we could meet with him to see the building. A week later we did. The minute I walked into the place, I knew this was it! Lynn looked at me and nodded. "You know, I think you're right." There was a huge room. I could visualize how I wanted to set up the rooms. There would be a receptionist area, waiting room, offices, three counseling rooms, the ultra sound room and the baby boutique room. I knew God was here and this was it!

We did look at another place, but I knew we wanted the one on Main Street. I told Linda. She was very happy, but her time was winding down. She was in the last weeks of work, so she concentrated on goodbyes and her new journey in her life. We gave her a wonderful send off party. A week before, we gave a party for the bookkeeper, Ann, who was stepping down after ten years. So here was me—the new Executive Director. I was beginning to form a plan! I was a little nervous with this role as Executive Director. It was big and came with different responsibilities than I had in

Chicago. But I felt up to the challenge because I knew God was in this with me.

I was planning Board meetings and talking with other Board Members. I told them about the building in Willimantic and they were excited to see it. I made an appointment with the landlord. They met Jerry and walked around the building. I told them the plan I had for the building. We took pictures for the Board Members that couldn't make it. We continued working at the little Center in Storrs. It was open one night a week. It was a church connected to a business, but the location was not very good—and it was only one room. I told the Board it wasn't working out, so they agreed to do away with it. The Board continued to pray about the building in Willimantic—whether or not to go forward with it. A month later I received a phone call from Jerry, the landlord. He said we needed to make a decision, because someone else was interested in the building. I asked Jerry to give me a week to let him know. He was very kind and agreed. I called the Board Members and said we needed to have an emergency meeting about the building in Willimantic. We met with some of the Board Members. Pastor Mike said he got the "thumbs up" from the ones that couldn't be there.

As we prayed for an answer, one of our volunteers, Pat, knocked on the door. She said she had a client thinking about having an abortion and needed to talk with someone. I told her that I would be right there. Before I left, I explained to the Board, "This is why we need to be in Willimantic!"

I wasn't there for the vote. Pastor Mike came down later and said, "Go ahead, call Jerry. Let him know we'll be renting the building." I was excited to tell Jerry. He was very happy. I told Jerry my ideas about putting up walls and adding rooms. He had no problem with it at all. We told Jerry, when we first met, how we planned to use the building. I told him who we were, what we did and what we did not do. He was excited to see something so positive in his community. Before Linda left, I invited Jerry to one of the banquets. He came to the banquet and made a large donation. He told me that all the great things we were doing for women and men in our communities just touched his heart.

I met with some of the volunteers and people interested in helping us turn this building into beautiful warm inviting locale where women and men could go in their crisis pregnancies. The first check was from a volunteer. This started the ball rolling. Geoff was laid off from the Railroad during this time. I asked if he would help build up the Center.

"What do you want to do?" he asked. "Where do you want everything? How big do you want it?" I told him what I wanted. He measured and figured it out and told me how much lumber, nails and other stuff we needed. So I emailed the information to staff, volunteers, Board Members—and everyone that supported us. Anyone who offered help—in prayer or financially—was informed as to what God was doing. I gave full details of what we needed each week. We received the money we needed to get the Center up and running! One of our volunteers called it a "Beg-O-Gram." I guess he was right, but God was moving in the hearts of people to bring in the needed funds.

Geoff rounded up help from the guys at Baptist Fellowship and other companies. Whenever we needed them—boom— they were there. A volunteer told me about a furniture store that gave gift cards to non-profits. We received a gift card donation for furniture. I chose some really nice tables, couch and a loveseat. People donated office desks, file cabinets, table and chairs for the break room. Others donated money for drywall and paint. Baptist Fellowship donated a huge copy machine. We received computers. A few people donated money toward a counter for the receptionist area. Once we were set up, people brought in baby clothes, diapers and stuff from the other Center. One lady donated toilet paper, soap and paper towels each month.

The best thing was the wonderful working relationship we had with the Town. Inspectors and the Fire Marshal checked to make sure we were doing things right and up to code. They were always pleased with the work, but the best thing was telling them what we were all about and what we planned to do—and their response. "Boy we sure need something like that is this town!"

Before we closed up the walls in the counseling rooms, I wanted to have staff, volunteers and Board Members write stuff on the walls. It would be on the inside of the dry walls—the side that did not show. We had scripture and encouraging words, praying that our clients would make good choices. As I contributed my own words on the walls in each counseling room, I prayed that The Gospel of Jesus Christ would be told here and many would come to trust Christ as their Savior and choose life for their babies. I wrote, "If anyone needs help from past abortions, they will find help here." When we were done, we prayed together.

After they were finished writing, they left. Geoff and some guys put up the walls. I walked around looking at what people had written. They were love notes to God! It just blessed my soul! The walls were up and in a few days, the painting was done. I wanted pictures for the walls. The daughter of Helen, a Board Member, was at a store and saw them throwing pictures and frames into the dumpster. She talked with the store manager about the pictures. He told her she could have them.

My first assumption was that the pictures were probably ripped and torn. Helen told me they were really nice. She said that we could go over to her daughter's house and look at them. I was pleasantly surprised to see so many in perfect condition—and absolutely gorgeous. Most of them had glass—not one was broken. "Take what you want, Pati," she said. I pictured the rooms where they would go. We piled them into my truck. I thanked them for the huge blessing!

When I got to the Center, Geoff helped me unload them. "What the heck are you going to do with all these pictures?" he asked.

As I started go through the pictures, it hit me! "Isn't this what we are doing here, Geoff? We rescue the broken hearted—help women and men that have been thrown aside by their families because of decisions they made or are thinking about making!" I think that Jesus was using the Crisis Pregnancy Centers to restore lives, bring hope and put their broken lives back together. They will come to realize what beautiful creatures they are and what beautiful babies that they are carrying, created by God to be used for His Glory. Where others thought trash, we saw beauty. We were seeing them through God's eyes!

The pictures went up. The furniture was placed where I wanted it, and the offices were taking shape. Another Board Member, Nicole, bought a bunch of curtains for the windows. We chose the ones that went with the colors we had on the walls.

Nicole and I both had a heart to see women healed from past abortions. She is an amazing woman and took her family each year to the March for Life in Washington, D.C. She always had a little one in tow, which was not easy, especially when she was scheduled as a Speaker. That God for a wonderful carrying husband to help with all of this. She is a good friend.

Before the Center opened the doors, the Board of Directors, staff, volunteers, many local church members and Pastors came to pray for the Center. We prayed in each room. We went outside and prayed in front of the building. Later, we found we sure did need it. With trained volunteers and staff was ready—and we knew that God was already ready—on September 28, 2009 we opened the doors for the very first time at Care Net Pregnancy Center of NECT, Willimantic, Connecticut. "May Jesus Christ be lifted up in this place and God be glorified."

I told the volunteers and staff I expected this would be very slow starting. Sometimes it takes a long while for people to realize there is a Center in the area. I didn't want them to be discouraged. We had to leave it in God's hands.

We only had to be obedient—and patient. It was a slow start. The churches and people in the area slowly realized who we were and what we did. I went to a couple of schools, spoke with school nurses and gave out brochures. I told them what we did and did not do. I was very pleased with the responses we got.

Thirteen months later, I received a phone call from Pastor Mike, telling me people were going to picket us. I expected this to happen, because we were right on Main Street— only a few blocks from a college and 20 minutes from a major University. I called the rest of the Board, but only two could make it. We decided to greet the picketers with hot chocolate and freshly baked chocolate chip cookies. We'd see what would happen.

Gail Z and Pastor Mike showed up with me. While we waited for them, we prayed. One of the volunteers was checking through the windows frequently. "Pati, they are here. They are outside!"

I peeked out the window and, sure enough, there they were holding their signs and handing papers to people as they walked by. They motioned drivers to blow their car horns to support them.

Pastor Mike walked out the door first, "What's your beef with us?" he asked.

"You don't refer or do abortions. You're not helping the whole woman," the picketer complained.

Pastor Mike explained what we did and didn't do. They wouldn't listen. "What school are you in?" he asked quietly. "What do you plan to do after college?" He made an effort to talk with some of them about Jesus Christ.

They wouldn't listen. He offered them hot chocolate and cookies—no takers!

When he came in, Gail Z went out for a few minutes. "Why are you out here?" she asked them. She got the same response as Pastor Mike. Gail pointed out how their mothers chose life for them. She explained what God said about abortion—and who Jesus is. They wouldn't hear it. And still no takers for hot chocolate and cookies.

Gail Z came back inside. I waited 10 minutes before I went out to speak to them. "Would you like to come in and see what we do?" I invited. "I'd be more than happy to show you around. You can come in and get warm."

"No!" And still no takers for hot chocolate and cookies.

We learned a lot as we watched the picketers. We knew we had to keep going on what God had called us to do. We prayed for the students. After an hour or so they left, one by one, until they were all gone.

This experience was a real eye opener about all the good and great things we were doing—and how the "other side" couldn't stand who we were and what we stood for. We stood for Jesus Christ and life! The rest of the year went by with no more picketers—just helping our clients and seeing God work.

It was April the following year when I heard one of our volunteers, talking to herself as she came through the waiting room into my office. "They're back!!" she whispered.

I knew who she was talking about. "Well, here we go again," I said. "Okay Lord, what do you want me to do?" I felt the need to speak with them. There were about 10 of them holding signs. "Fake Clinic," "No Choice Here," "They Tell Lies," "Against Abortion."

When I went out to talk to them, my Director of Development and her three-month old baby came with me. "Why are you guys picketing the Center?" I asked.

They shouted, "You are a fake clinic! You lie! You don't do abortions or refer for an abortion! You don't help the whole woman, you give them no choice!"

I said, "No, we don't refer for abortions—and no, we don't do abortions—and yes we do give them a choice. But what I can do is show you what we do." Again I extended the invitation. "If you would like to come into the Center, I'd happy to show you around."

One girl said, "I've already been in there as a client!"

I stopped for a moment and looked at her. "Yeah. I think I remember you."

She got put off when I said that and walked away holding her sign and yelling at cars to honk their horns.

Then a lady said, "Well, I've never been in there. I'll come in." When she came in, I showed her around the Center. I showed her what the clients fill out before we see them. I told her, "We talk to our clients about Jesus Christ." I took her into my office, the counseling rooms and the break room. I showed her where we'd put the ultra sound machine when we got it. "Our other Center has an ultra sound machine," I said.

Something interesting happened. When she walked into the baby boutique, she did what every woman does. I could hear it under her breath. "Aww."

We returned to the waiting room. I explained the movie we were showing throughout the day. "We give the movie to our clients who aren't sure what they want to do about their baby," I told her. "We give out popcorn to the clients with the movie, and tell them they can keep the movie, or give it to someone else who may need to see it.

"We also ask them to let us know what they think of the movie." I kept talking. "We ask what decision they made. We tell them we'd love them, no matter what they decided." I gave her a copy of the movie and three bags of popcorn.

She said, "No. Please keep that for your clients."

I thought that was an interesting statement! "You kept saying very faintly, 'I didn't know.'" I said. "What didn't you know?" She told me she didn't realize we did all this. Then I switched gears on her. "Are you going to college?" I asked.

"Yes, I want to be a lawyer someday."

"Wow, that is great! When did you decide you wanted to become a lawyer?"

"Oh, when I was a little girl around ten or so," she smiled.

"Could you have litigated a case when you were ten?"

She looked at me as if I had lost my mind. "Are you kidding me? No way," she said.

"How come?" I asked her.

"Because I wasn't educated yet!"

"Well, Bingo!" I said. "I just educated you on what Crisis Pregnancy Centers do." She stood there shaking her head.

Before she left, I asked her if I could give her a hug. As she walked toward me she said, "Yes." She thanked me for the tour of the Center, the movie and popcorn for everyone. She promised to share it with her friends outside.

The most interesting part of the day may have been when this young woman came in to see what we did. But that was not it. The interesting part was, when I looked out the window. Her friends gathered around her to see what she had. But that wasn't it either—it was what she didn't do. She never picked up her sign again! When she walked away someone else was holding it. I believe we helped educate her, loved her where she was and prayerfully, God got hold of her heart as we walked through the Center. I believe that is how to help the people that don't like what we do—educate and love them. They will see Jesus Christ in our compassion for them. Who will have compassion for them, if we don't?

Remember how we prayed in front of the building before we opened the Center for the first time? God knew that the sidewalk and our Center would be a huge target. We needed to be prayed up and prepared for battle! Every Crisis Pregnancy Center that turns the key to open its doors each day is turning that key into a battle field of Life and Death— eternal and physical. The jobs are hard, but when you're called to this great ministry, God will prepare you. He will not call you and then drop you. I had to remind myself on a daily basis. I called Executive Director friends often. I called Lisa M several times. I'd tell her, "I'm quitting! I can't take it anymore." Then she would calm me down until I realized that she was right and I was wrong.

A month would go by and it was her turn to call me saying that she was quitting, and couldn't take it anymore! Then I would be the one saying, "Now Lisa, didn't you tell me to chill and I would be fine?"

There were lots of times I called Donnita, another Executive Director friend. She was always a source of encouragement like Lisa M. The three of us met for coffee and prayer. Donnita was very dedicated to her job and always had a smile on her face. Linda C was another Executive Director I called. She had a way with her that would put you at ease. She was the one I asked questions about our Post-Abortion Recovery Program. She wrote the book to help other women and men step out of the pain, shame and guilt, and find healing and restoration. It was great we could call each other and be there for one another.

The days that were hard for me were the days when I grew to what God had called me to do. Our Center struggled to just keep up with the bills and pay the staff. Some months were better than others. We had our Annual Fund Raising Banquet, our Hike for Life and our Christmas Appeal Letter, which helped so much—but it was the other days that were hard. I knew these two Centers were God's Centers and not mine. Sometimes when I became discouraged, God would remind me of all the lives that these two Centers touched—the lives that were changed, lives that were restored, babies that were born, women and men's lives changed—lives that trusted Jesus Christ. Then there were the communities that could see something great was happening behind these doors.

Wasn't I ready for this? When I started I wasn't sure, but year after year, I knew God was taking care of me. Many times I'd say, "Not ready for this!"

All I had to do was trust in God. A quote from Martin Luther King Jr. reminded me, "…taking the first step, even when you don't see the whole staircase!" I was doing that.

XVII

DID YOU SAY GOD'S GOT IT?

The beginning of the year my dad was not doing well. He was sick, and then he got better. Weeks later he was sick again. My brothers and I visited him more and more often. When Geoff and I visited, he talked a bit, but then was extremely tired. He couldn't get out of bed without the help of the nurse aides. They cleaned, dressed and got him ready for his day. They put him in his favorite chair. To him that was a busy and exhausting day.

When he first moved back from Florida, Dad had his own apartment. He was very independent, living on his own and driving his car—for a long time. Each year he seemed to get a little slower and need more help. My brothers found him a great place where he had a little cottage and could walk to the main building and the main dining room. He made his own breakfast and lunch and had dinner delivered. After a few bouts of pneumonia, he was put into a rehab center. After a time, he went back to his little cottage. One more time with pneumonia got him into the hospital, then back to the rehab center. The doctors told us he needed 24-hour care. Because he was already a resident with his little cottage, he was able to get a room in the nursing home part.

When we told him he was being transferred to one room in the nursing care facility, he took it well. He brought his favorite chair and dressing table, got a brand new TV and table. We put family pictures all around him, so it would feel like home. When we were putting up the pictures, he had a look of sadness on his face. He made sure he had Mom's engagement picture right next to him. The look on his face as he looked at Mom's picture brought tears to my eyes.

Geoff and I visited on weekends. Dad talked about his old Navy days and his 40+ years working on the railroad. He always had model railroads. When he moved out of his little cottage, he donated his model railroad to the Senior Community where he was living. He wanted others to enjoy it. Moving the model took a huge effort by family members and staff from the Senior Place. Once it was relocated, Dad was very happy. I had a lot of respect for my dad. That took a lot for him to do—he had model engines that he bought in the 60s—some even earlier.

One weekend Geoff and I went to see him. When we entered his room, we went over to give him a kiss and say, "Hi." He was fine with me. When Geoff approached him, Dad's eyes got big. He pushed back in his chair and looked as if he had no idea who Geoff was. He got very agitated. Geoff was upset and fought back the tears that filled his eyes.

"Dad, I said, "This is Geoff, my husband, your son-in-law. Don't you recognize him?"

He mumbled, "Yes," but seemed unsure. We stayed and tried to talk with him, but it seemed like he was really not there anymore. I talked and he listened. I showed him Mom's picture. He smiled and said, "Pati, that is your mother!"

"I know Dad," I told him. "She is very pretty."

"Yes, she is," he said.

Dad was slipping away, and it broke my heart to see him like this. This was the man who worked two jobs to keep a nice home and food on the table. We had annual family vacations. Dad worked around the house, planted flowers in his garden and played with his model railroad. He never missed seeing my brothers' baseball games. Dad enjoyed playing catch with my brothers or watching me march with the high school baton squad. He made sure to take us to church every Sunday. Dad took great pride in making sure the American Flag was put up on July 4th and Memorial Day and taking his children ice-skating. He loved his job on the railroad in New Haven. He was our dad, who was there for all of us, loving his family. The thought of him leaving me was too much to bear.

My brother Tony called me on Monday, March 15th. "Dad doesn't look good at all," he told us.

"Geoff and I were just there yesterday. He wasn't doing too well then," I agreed. I knew I had to go see him again. I told my staff at the Center I was taking the day off to see my dad.

When Geoff and I got there, the nurse saw us. "He can't talk," she said confidentially, "but he can still hear you."

Just the day before, he was attempting to talk with me. The change was so fast. I pulled a chair up to the side of the bed. We were face-to-face. All of a sudden I felt like I needed to tell him it was okay to go and be with Jesus and Mom. So that is what I did. I told him, "You are a great daddy, and you were a wonderful, loving and caring husband. You took care of Mom when she was sick with Parkinson's disease. You've been a wonderful father-in-law and grandfather—and a terrific great grandfather. You took good care of Robert, Tony—and me.

"Daddy, I will miss you so much, but Jesus and Mom are waiting for you. It's okay to go. You did your job with all of us, and now your job is done. Your body is just worn out. It's time to go, Daddy."

I held his hand, kissed him on the cheek and told him how much I loved him. In the corner of my eye, I noticed Geoff had left the room. I sat there quoting scripture, telling Dad I loved him.

Geoff came back into the room, gave Dad a kiss on his forehead and held his hand. I could see tears in my husband's eyes. I knew he loved my daddy. "Pati, honey we need to go." He took my hand. "You know we can't stay here all night."

I knew he was right, but this was my daddy! I gave Dad another kiss, held his hand, and told him I loved him so much. I learned later that my brothers that evening told him it was okay to go.

The next morning around 5:30 my brother Tony called me to tell me Dad just died. I knew it was going to happen. But those words—those words—dug into my heart. I thought I had prepared myself, but—it doesn't happen that way. I told my brother we would be there in an hour. Within the hour we were in Meriden. When we got there, my brothers were in the living room area and when they saw us coming down the hall, they greeted us with hugs and tears. I hugged them both like I wasn't ever going to let them go.

We walked into Dad's room, and he was still there. My brother called the funeral home and told them to pick him up. I stood there and cried. My daddy was gone! But then I thought—no more pain, no more missing Mom—and he was with Jesus and my mom. What a great place to be!

Geoff called the boys. They said it would take two days to get there from Florida. When they all got to Connecticut, I was happy to see bright little shining faces, so innocent and happy to see us. The children came up to me and started hugging, some of them crying. They said they loved me and were very sad that Great Grandpa died. But in the same breath, they said, "But Grandma! Great Grandpa is with Jesus now!" My sons hugged me and told me they loved me. Both my daughters-in-laws hugged and told me they loved me.

Dad had a military funeral. It was a sad day. When I saw my husband, two sons and nephew carry Dad's coffin into the church, I lost it. Dad carried us for so long, as kids—and now his family was carrying him.

After the service my brothers walked with me down the aisle in tears. I had not seen my brother's cry like that since we were very little. We got into the limousine. It was a long ride to the gravesite.

In the early 1900s my grandfather purchased gravesites for the family. That's where my dad was laid to rest—next to my mom, his beloved wife, grandparents and uncle. It was a cold, windy day, but the sun was shining brightly. When we were at the gravesite, at one point during the service we were told to cover our ears—especially the grandkids—because they were going to do the three-gun salute. Emily sat on my lap. She and all the kids had their hands over their ears. We heard the gunshot three times and it was done. But Emily, still holding her hands over her ears, in her "outside voice" asked, "Grandma did the shooting stop?"

That broke the tension and everyone had a little chuckle. My granddaughter, Ella, told her daddy, Michael, that she just wanted to see Great Grandpa. "Couldn't he just come out of that box?" she asked. "I am very sad." She scrubbed away the tears.

Granddaughter Natalie buried her face in her daddy's arms and cried. The rest of the kids stood there with tears and sadness in their eyes.

My heart broke. I wanted so much to have Dad see these precious children grow up. I wished Mom were there, too, to see her great grandchildren, and how her grandsons were all grown up—and their beautiful families.

After the graveside services, we headed back to Meriden. We had a nice meal at a local Country Club. It was lovely to have the whole family together—our sons, my brothers and their families. I couldn't remember the last time we were all together, but I was cherishing this time. I really missed my family a lot.

Geoff and I had talked about moving back to Florida to be with our sons and their families. They loved the idea.

During this time of the passing of my dad, the whole family stayed with us. We had three bedrooms and 13 people. But we had fun!

The kids wanted to play outside, but it was much too cold. Beth decided to let the kids run around for 10 or 15 minutes, to get their pent-up energy out. By the time they came back into the house, we had little red faces and some runny noses to deal with. But they were so darn cute!

So it was hot chocolate time and we sat around the dining room table, chatting. I loved it! I was in Grandma Heaven!!!

We talked about how Geoff and I should move back to Florida to be with everyone. The more we talked, the better it sounded. Geoff was working temporary jobs. My job, on the other hand—I really had to know if God was moving us or was I moving us. I knew that God would let us know what to do. He always had.

After they left I was so sad. The grandkids cried. They didn't want to leave us. Our house was so empty. I missed them—and Dad. A few days later, I called Gail Z, a real good friend of mine. We prayed together a lot, and she had good advice for me. It always seemed to line up with scripture. I told her I was thinking about moving back to Florida. She wasn't surprised. As a matter of fact, at the next Board meeting, I was told they could see it all over my face.

"Is it that obvious?" I asked them.

They said "Yep!" I knew how the past Executive Director, Linda, felt when she wanted to leave—but who would replace her? I knew the two Centers were God's. I had to leave it in His hands. I knew God was going to take care of me.

One of my friends, Lisa M, and I were going to meet with Donnita, to have coffee and pray together. We found these times to be excellent sources of encouragement. Lisa M picked me up and while we were on the way to the meeting Beth called. I chatted with her for a few minutes. "Mom, "she said, "I wish you could find a job down here doing what you are doing in Connecticut." I agreed that would be really nice.

I repeated what Beth told me, and Lisa M overheard what I said.

"Pati," she said. "I know someone that wants to move back to Connecticut. She is an Executive Director in Florida. I'm not sure where her Center is located."

Beth overheard what Lisa said and was amazed. It took my breath away for a few seconds. I told Beth I'd find out where it was, and let her know. After Beth and I completed our call, I looked at Lisa M and said, "Are you kidding me?" I could hardly believe it.

Lisa M laughed. "No, I'm not kidding you. I don't know the particulars, but I will find out for you."

A few weeks later she called me to tell about Gail P. She was in Orlando, Florida.

"Orlando?" Then, not caring about the answer, I continued. "Well, at least it isn't that far from Jacksonville!" I learned later that "Gail P, from Orlando" was going to the Care Net conference we were planning to attend. It was hard to comprehend all of this.

At the Conference in Orlando I sat with my Executive Director friends and some of my staff. Lisa M pointed Gail P. out to me. I went over to introduce myself.

She said, "Oh yes, Pati. I heard about you—and we need to talk!" During the conference, we found a quiet area and talked for about two hours. We were amazed at how this could work out for each of us. She wanted to move back to Connecticut to be with family and I wanted to move to Florida to be with my family. We were in awe of what God was doing.

As I flew back from the Conference, I had much to think and pray about. When I got home I told Geoff. He was amazed too, at the possibility of moving back to be with our kids. "Pati," he said, "this is amazing, but we don't have the money to move right now."

"Yeah, I know," I agreed.

Then we said, "Let's see what God will do."

Geoff said the only way we could save money was if we didn't have to pay rent. So I told him I was going to ask our landlords if we could not pay rent for a few months. Geoff told me, "You are definitely crazy to do this! This is the craziest idea you've ever had." But the more I prayed, the more I felt it was right to do.

We were renting our house from a wonderful Christian couple. I called her. "I know this is an off-the-wall question— you may think I have totally lost my mind— but I've been praying and feel at least I need to ask you." I took a deep breath and jumped in. "Could we stay in your house for the next few months or so and not pay any rent?" I continued, "We will still keep up with the utilities and water. We're trying to move back to Florida to be with our family and this is the only way we could save money to do it."

She said, "Oh my! Well, let me talk it over with my husband. We'll pray about it too, and I'll let you know. Okay?"

"Sure," I breathed. "We'll all be praying—and thank you!" I hung up the phone. "That didn't go so bad, did it, Geoff?" I smiled. "Let's see what God will do!' Geoff thought I was nuts even to ask. "All they can say is 'no' or 'yes.'" I felt I at least needed to ask her.

A week later I called her back. I was on pins and needles, as I listened to her phone ringing, then she picked up the phone. "We talked it over," she said, "prayed about it—and decided 'yes' we'll to do this for you guys. Our end will be very tight, but you told me that you wanted to move back to be with your family, and this is the only way you can save money. So again," she continued, "yes, we'll do this." I thanked her over and over and over again for helping us get back with our kids and grandkids. When I got off the phone, I told Geoff what they said and his chin just about hit the floor. He couldn't believe they were going to do something like this for us. So at the beginning of each month, instead of writing the check for the rent, we put it in our savings account. We told our sons and their families and they were very excited. We told them we planned to be in Florida by March.

But plans changed—God was moving!!

Our landlords called a few months later and told us they had to move back into their house by mid-December, so that put us three months early. Geoff Jr. told us we could move in with them—they had an extra bedroom. So with that blessing, we knew it was only a matter of time. Gail P, the Executive Director from Orlando, told me she was coming up to visit her family for Thanksgiving.

I told the Board and suggested they interview her. The Board Members started to pray. Gail P thought it was a good idea. She had a great interview with the Board and after she left, I told them she had been an Executive Director longer than me. I told the Board she'd take the Centers to the next level—a new journey. They voted and decided to hire her. I was very happy for her—but sad for me. I knew that she would so a wonderful job.

Gail P told the Board she wouldn't be able to start until February, so from mid- December to February, there'd be no Executive Director. There were, however, two Center Directors, and I knew they'd pick up the work until she arrived. This was, by far, the hardest job I ever had to leave. I absolutely loved my job! But I knew my time was winding down and God had other plans for me.

Before I left, some of the area Executive Directors got together to give me a little send off. I was happy and appreciated that they took time off from their busy schedules at their Centers to say goodbye to me! I told them I was going to miss them, their prayers and their support for me when sometimes, I wanted to quit! We laughed at that one, because we all did the same thing. As we said goodbye, I started to cry. These ladies knew how hard it was to let go of this ministry. But they also knew—as I did—that God calls you in—and then He calls you out to do something else for Him.

A few days later, I began to clean up for Gail P. I shook my head, as I saw all the papers and junk I kept in my "some day I will need them drawer." I chided myself, "Pati Adams, you've got to stop doing this!" Some paper was needed, some was not. Some volunteers gave me personal going away gifts, which touched my heart. I was going to miss them—they were the gifts God had given me, to help me with this work. Each one of them brought special talents and gifts with them. What pure joy it was to work side-by-side with these great people!

My staff, some Board members and volunteers got together to give me a going-away breakfast. There was a cute little hometown café that opened across from the Danielson Center. They told me how much I'd be missed and asked me to let them know what God was doing in my life. They gave me two pieces of jewelry—a gorgeous necklace and bracelet matched set! Those were very hard goodbyes. I'd been with most of them for three years. We prayed, cried and laughed together.

The day before we were to move, the Board of Directors had a going-away breakfast for me, too. After eating, we sat and visited for a while. Then one-by-one they left to start their day.

These people took a chance on me and hired me. They were praying people who loved the Lord. They were Board Members that listened to their Executive Director—and I was the Executive Director that listened to them. We worked together very well.

I really loved them. It was an honor to serve, and a pleasure to see Jesus Christ working in them. They had such a heart for the unborn, the moms and dads that were in a crisis pregnancy, women and men hurting from past abortions. But most important was sharing the Gospel of Jesus Christ!

The Willimantic Center was closed that day, so I decided to go back alone and say goodbye. I felt it was my final voyage. While I was there the phone rang. I was Larry, with a group that I worked with for two years. They were helping us get an ultrasound machine for the Center. I spoke at their fund raising banquets, picnic fundraisers and many other events to help get this ultrasound. Larry said they knew I was moving to Florida, but wanted to see me before I left.

I called Lynn, a volunteer that lived close by to come to the Center. When she arrived she asked what was going on. I told her Larry was coming in to see me before I left and I didn't think it was appropriate to be alone with a man when the Center was closed.

Larry arrived—beaming from head to toe. "Pati," he began, "first, I am so glad I caught you before you moved! I wanted to give you this before you left. You've been working with us for so long—we thought it was appropriate to give this check to you. You can order your new ultrasound for this Center!!" He continued, "We have all the money raised, but we could only start with the funds needed to order the ultrasound machine. The final payment will be available in a few weeks." I couldn't believe my eyes and ears. I was overwhelmed. The tears started to flow—again! "Pati, it was a pleasure to work with you on this project and you will be truly missed," Larry smiled as he handed me the check.

I gave him a hug. "Oh, it was such a pleasure to work with you all. Many babies' lives will be saved because of the time—countless hours you put into this." They had such huge hearts for our precious clients. "Thank you so much, Larry. I can never thank you enough. I hope I can get back to see you and the new ultra sound," I said. We hugged goodbye and he left.

Lynn was very excited. "Wow, this is truly amazing!" She had tears in her eyes. She gave me a long hug and told me to keep in touch.

I sat in what had been my office for another few minutes and cried. I was so overwhelmed that God would do this for me this day of all days. Sometimes I wondered if I did a good job for Him—but I felt in my heart that God was pleased. I held the check, walked around each room and thanked Him for women and men that chose life for their babies. I thanked Jesus Christ that they found the true healing for their abortions. I thanked God for all the blood, sweat and tears that went into this Center to build these rooms. I thanked Him for the people that financially gave from their hearts, the staff, Board Members and volunteers that helped with painting and construction to get this Center up and running. I prayed Gail P, the new Executive Director, would take these two Centers to the next level—and for Him to watch over her and her family.

Before I walked out the door, I called my friend and Treasurer of our Board of Directors, Gail Z and told her about the check and where I would leave it. "Well, Pati," she said, "it seems God is giving you a good send-off. I believe He is pleased at your work here for the past three years! This is very exciting news!"

"I think you're right," I agreed. "And it feels great that I did a good job for Him." I told her I'd call Pastor Mike and let him know about the check, too. When I called him, he was very excited and told me I'd be missed greatly. After I got off the phone, I grabbed a little box with some of my things in it, and my purse, and walked into the room where the ultrasound would be housed, thinking of all the precious little ones that God is going to save with this ultrasound. I remembered the Danielson Center had an ultra sound and my nurse who asked me to come with her and see the ultrasound she was going to do on a client. The client was shaking, nervous and saying, "This is not a baby." But when she was asked if she wanted to see the screen she said, "Yes." When she gazed upon the screen, she couldn't stop crying. My nurse explained to her what she was looking at. She kept saying, "That's my baby, that's my baby! What was I thinking?" Tears just flowed from her eyes as she said to us, "Thank you for showing me what I was about to destroy." She got up and made an appointment to come back. I could hear her saying, "Thank God, Thank God!"

So there I was, standing in this room where this new ultrasound would be installed, and I thanked God for this room and what He was going to do here. I turned off the lights, locked the door and got into my car. I felt good that Jesus Christ was pleased with me.

Next day was moving day—again!!! We got help from our church's Baptist Fellowship. They quickly packed up the truck. Even though Geoff and I loaded some stuff in the truck the day before, we were glad for the help.

When we were done, we gathered around the front yard and they prayed for a safe and pleasant trip.

XVIII

I DIDN'T SEE THAT COMING!

Geoff and I left early the next morning. I was happy that I didn't have to follow in his truck. I rode with him in the rental truck, towing my car on the trailer. Geoff's truck had given up. Before we moved, a guy was driving up and down our neighborhood looking for cars or trucks. He saw Geoff's truck and knocked on our door. He asked Geoff if his truck was for sale. We looked at each other in amazement. Geoff told him the truck didn't run, but the guy didn't care. He asked how much he wanted for it, and handed him cash!! Geoff signed over the title, help put the truck on his trailer and away it went, just like that! We were sort of sad to see it go. It was brand new when we bought it and gave it to Michael when he was going to Bible College. There were memories with that truck. It was the same truck that lost the heat when Michael went to pick up Beth. It was the truck that Michael and Beth took on their honeymoon. We were amazed that this guy showed up at our front door to buy the truck just as we were talking about what to do with it!

The car we were towing was given to me by one of my volunteers because my car stopped working and needed a new motor. It was too old for that expense. That was a sad day. It was a 1995 SLS Cadillac—pearl white—with white interior. My car died before Geoff's truck. I was an Executive Director with no car, wondering how I would get to work. Before his truck died, Geoff drove me to work, and my sweet volunteers drove me home. God was watching out for me!

We made it to Baltimore, Maryland when it started to snow, so we called it a night. The next morning the sun was up and the snow was gone. We were on our way to Florida. We called the kids to let them know when we'd be at the storage shelter to unload our stuff. A few Christian Bikers friends, our two sons and the grandkids met us. Our granddaughters helped with a couple things—and then they were pretty much done. The stuff was too heavy for me, so we girls hung out together. Our grandson Will was a huge help. It was good to be back with our kids and their families. Geoff and I felt really blessed. After we settled down at Geoff Jr.'s house it was time to find work.

A friend of ours asked Geoff if he would help him fix a lawn mower. Geoff told him he'd help but couldn't spend too much time because he was putting out resumes. Geoff checked out the lawn mower. He went to lawn mower store to get the parts he needed. He saw a pair of sunglasses he liked and tried them on. The guy behind the counter said,

"Hey, those look pretty good on you. Do you want to add them to your purchase?"

"No, not right now," Geoff said. "I don't have a job yet. I'm getting the parts for a friend."

"Are you looking for a job?" the man asked.

"Yes, I am," Geoff answered.

"Why don't you apply here?" he suggested. "I think they're looking for someone."

Geoff was a little surprised but filled out the application, had an interview the next week and was hired! He was happy to have no more applications to fill out. "Thank you, Jesus!" he prayed. "Thank you for the job!"

I had sent my resume to the Pregnancy Center in Orlando and they told me they'd be calling me soon. I never heard back from them. So I just moved on.

One day, when the weather was getting warm, I couldn't find any shorts to wear. I remembered Beth telling me about a Thrift Store, so I took a ride to see if I could find it. I found the place and what I was looking for, plus some other items. I thought while I was looking for a job, maybe I could volunteer. I spoke with one of the owners and to my amazement they were looking for help—paid help! They asked for my resume. After I made my purchase, I went home, returned with my resume and got the job! Geoff and I both got jobs on the same day. When God moves, He sure does move!

We were excited to be employed. It wasn't exactly what we were looking for, but we knew it was where God wanted us. Before I left the Center in Connecticut, the Board asked me if I would be their Guest Speaker at their banquet the following May. I was so honored. I told them I wasn't sure if I was the right person to speak. Gail Z argued, "Pati, you have a great story to tell. Yes, we've had people who were well-known speak at our banquets, but you are just as good as they are." She continued, "I think people will really relate to you because of your background and what you've been through."

At first I was shocked that someone wanted me to speak. Then I thought maybe she was right. Maybe I can touch someone or his or her family with my story. I was in awe of what God was doing. A few weeks later, I received a call from the group that got the ultrasound for the Willimantic Center. They found out I was speaking at the banquet in May and wanted to wait until I arrived to dedicate the ultrasound. They planned to make the dedication the weekend I was there. I told them, they didn't have to wait for me. Larry said, "Pati, we worked with you for almost two years—and we want you to be a part of this." I thanked him, accepted the invitation, and told him it would be an honor to be there. He said, "Wonderful! We'll see you when you get here." All I could do was cry.

During this time Geoff Jr. and his family were considering a move out of town. Other family members owned a business and needed help. We moved to Florida to be with family and suddenly they might be moving.

"Okay, God," I prayed. "What is going on here? Didn't You hear I was happy living near my kids and their families?" I loved being around my granddaughter, who I got to see every day—morning and night. We ate dinner, watched TV and played games with her. It was nice to come home, have dinner with family. I knew I would miss that. A few weeks later, we found out they really were moving.

Geoff and I had to find a place to live—fast. It was a very sad day when Geoff Jr and his family moved—and hard to believe! They were moving about four hours away. But for Geoff and me it was too far. The day arrived. We hugged and kissed and told them we'd miss them. I told Geoff Jr. to call us when they got there safe and sound.

About a month earlier, when we found out Geoff Jr was moving, I asked Michael and Beth if we could move in with them, just until we found a place. They said, "Sure, we'd love to have you guys stay here with us."

When we moved in with Michael and his family, we had a welcoming committee at the front door. In the bedroom we were using, our grandkids had drawn us pictures and messages, "Welcome Home Grandma and Grandpa" and "We love you!" They were taped to the walls. It was so touching and so cute. At that time Michael and Beth had six kids— Emily, William, Abby, Ella, Joey, Lydia and number seven was on the way. Every time I came home from work, the children were at the door jumping up and down. Even their dog, Corey, was excited to see us. It was so nice to come home to every night.

When Geoff came home from work each day, his Harley could be heard from far away. All the kids knew Grandpa was coming home. They flung open the front door, jumped up and down on the front porch. Beth cooked great dinners and I did the clean up.

We gave Michael and Beth date nights once in awhile and we'd watch the kids. After a month of looking for an apartment or house to rent—we couldn't believe how much people wanted for rents—we had a real estate agent help us. She told us it might be cheaper to buy a house. We weren't really sure about doing that, but Geoff and I decided since this was our last move, maybe we should look into it. We saw "FORECLOSURE" signs everywhere. That was a huge eye-opener! We wanted three bedrooms, two bathrooms, pool, two-car garage and a fireplace.

We saw a several houses. They all had some kind of damage and would need lots of work to make them livable. Most of them were out of our price range. The real estate agent showed us a house that wasn't a foreclosure and had what I was praying for. It was just okay. Geoff and I talked about the house. He said, "Pati, it has everything we've been praying for—and it's not a foreclosure. Let's pray about it then go back with different eyes to see the house that has everything we want." I agreed to go back. We called our agent and she took us back to the house. When we got there, I decided I liked it a little more. It needed painting and cleaning, but Geoff said we could fix things one at a time. We told the kids we thought we found a house. Everyone was excited. Geoff and I made a down payment on the house, filled out some paper work and waited for the bank to approve us.

A few days later Michael and his family were out visiting friends when we got a call from Michael saying they were rushing Ella to the hospital. They wanted to make sure we were home, because he was dropping Beth and Ella at the Emergency Room and bringing the other kids home.

We were at the house when Michael dropped off the rest of the kids. The children were all upset, crying and asking what was happening to Ella. We told them, "Ella is in a great place. The doctors and nurses will take good care of her. We know that God will take care of her even more." We sat the children down and prayed for little Ella. It seemed to settle them down a bit. With worried and scared little grandkids, it was hard not to show my emotions to them. I knew God was taking care of Ella. Waiting was the hardest thing to do. Michael told us, when he dropped off the kids, that she was having trouble breathing.

We waited for a very long time and finally Michael called. He said that a fire ant had bitten Ella. The doctors thought maybe 20 or more bit her, but it was just one little fire ant! She was going into anaphylactic shock and her throat was closing up very quickly. The doctor said she would be okay, but the next time, they'd have a very small amount of time to get her to the emergency room. They were given two EpiPens in case an emergency came up. Michael said they'd bring Ella home in a few hours. The hospital personnel needed to monitor her for a little while longer.

Weeks later, Michael and Beth realized that staying in Florida was not going to work for them. Ella could not go outside to play with her brothers and sisters, because of the possibility of her getting bit again. We were devastated. Michael and Beth realized the possibilities of living in Florida were slowly slipping away. Michael had almost everything ready to be a Church Planter in Jacksonville. Things were changing fast. They looked at a map of the

United States to find where there were no fire ants. One state they both loved was Colorado, so they looked at Colorado Springs. Michael got in touch with some churches and they had the opportunity to go there. Geoff and I watched the six grandkids when Beth and Michael took the trip to check it out. We had a great time watching them, but by the end of the day, I was pooped!

When Michael and Beth returned a few days later, they knew Colorado was the place God was sending them. I knew they couldn't stay in Florida—we were all nervous about the possibility of Ella getting bit again. Every time she saw anything crawling, she cried.

I couldn't believe they were going to actually move so far away. They wanted us to come with them. But we had already started the ball rolling with buying the house. We thought about walking away from the deal, but we'd be losing a lot of money. At first we agreed if we lost it, we lost it. A few days later Geoff said, "Pati, we signed a contract saying we wanted to buy the house. I don't think we'd be honoring God if we tried to break it." I knew he was right. A few days later we received a phone call that we got the house.

It was kind of bittersweet for us. The house needed some work. Our friends, Allan and Maria did carpet work. We asked them to come over, look at the house and tell us how much it would be for new carpeting for the whole house. Allan measured and told us how much it would cost. We told them we wouldn't be able to do it for a few months so they took up the old carpet for us. Geoff sealed the cement floor and we put throw rugs on the floors.

A few months passed. We realized the money we needed for the flooring wasn't going to happen. We called to tell them, and they said for us to call when we could do it. They were so sweet to understand. We thanked God for Godly friends!

Before we moved in we painted the ceilings and walls. It started to look a lot better. But in the back of my mind—all the things we wanted, like the pool and big back yard was for our grandkids to enjoy. We even had a place for the swing set we were going to buy— but our sons and their families would not be here. We finally moved in and all the family came over to enjoy the pool and eat hamburgers. We were very careful with Ella. Someone would pick her up and put her into the pool. We told her not touch the sides of the pool. I was heartbroken for her. When she wanted to get out of the pool, someone carried her out and brought her to a chair on the porch. We kept watchful eyes around her for fire ants. It was very sad. We could see the other kids loving their flip-flops and running around the yard. Ella wore either cowboy boots or socks with her sneakers. She was a little trooper and had a positive attitude. They let her outside for a little bit, but it got too stressful for everyone, including little Ella, so she stayed in the house more than she went outside.

Moving day came for Michael and Beth. Geoff and I went over to help them pack the truck. There were many people from their church helping them. Everyone told them how much they'd be missed. Some of their friends said to us, "Wow, you guys just moved down here to be with all of your kids and grandkids, and now everyone is moving away! You guys must be very sad." I agreed with them. We were very sad. We knew God had a plan and we just needed to lean on Him. Watching the kids' stuff being put into the truck was hard—just like when Geoff Jr. and his family moved away. After the truck was loaded up Michael, Beth, the kids and Corey the dog, came over to spend the night at our house for the last time. The first thing the kids wanted to do was jump into the pool. It was kind of late, but everyone jumped in. We grilled burgers, and then everyone was very tired. So it was off to bed. In the morning, Michael wanted to get on the road early. They had a long journey ahead of them and were stopping to see friends along the way.

It was so hard for Geoff and me to say goodbye. We moved back to Florida to be with our families. Now they were leaving us. We asked them to call us when they got to Colorado. We hugged and kissed, and they all piled into the van. Corey the dog jumped in, too. They waved goodbye and in the blink of an eye, they were gone.

I buried myself in Geoff's arms as I had done so many other times. I missed our sons and their families already. Now what were we to do?

We heard from the kids when they made it safe and sound. They found a house after a few weeks, started with the church and were on their way to do what God called them to do. Geoff and I worked, took care of our house and went to church. After awhile I left my job because I felt it was time to go and see what God had for me again. I got a part-time job in a local Christian Book Store. I knew retail and it was close to my house. I was happy about the people

I was working with. I knew God was doing something in my life. I just had to be patient and lean on Him.

Michael and Beth's seventh baby was a girl. They named her Julianne. In 2014 they had their eighth baby, a boy named Peter!!

A few months later I saw one of the ladies in our church obviously struggling with some issues. I asked her, when she was by herself, if she ever had an abortion. She said, "Yes." I told her about a Post Abortion Recovery Program I went through that helped me. At first she said, "No way!" After we talked more about it, she said, "Yes." When she completed the program, I saw a big difference in her life. We became good friends.

A few more ladies from my church knew what I did. I could see something was going on with them. So I talked with them—not together. I told each of them there was another lady wanting to go through the program. I asked if they would agree to go through this together. They agreed. I met with them together.

Normally there are two facilitators, but this was not the case. It was hard for them at first. I watched these two precious ladies unfold before my eyes, digging through their pain and letting go. This is what I told them would happen before we started. "It is like looking at a beautiful lush green lawn, then all of sudden, up pops a dandelion. You can just mow over it and the grass will look as good as new. But then, in a week or even before, there it is again!" I told my ladies this program was standing over that dandelion with a shovel, and digging down to get at the root of it—and pulling it up— digging and yanking up all the pain, shame and guilt. That is the first six weeks. Then the next six weeks is the healing part. I explained that Jesus Christ was the one with the shovel. Jesus Christ was the one healing, not me.

I watched these two ladies— and the one before—and saw God working in their lives each week. Yes, tears did flow. The pain was very real—but the healing was the best part of their lives. It was nothing I did—it was all what Jesus Christ did!!

I also volunteered at a local Pregnancy Center that has a Post Abortion Recovery Program. There I saw three beautiful ladies that were hurting from past abortions and saw them become what God had created them to be. After I thought about the part that God allowed me to play, I knew if I'd moved away earlier, I would have missed out on why God wanted me to be here.

During the course of my time at the Center in Connecticut, I attended conferences. I had the pleasure of meeting ladies at these conferences that had the same heart I did with recovery. These women were very passionate about helping other women to find the healing and restoration we all found from our past abortions.

I guess I would say God has a plan for everyone. It may not be where I wanted to be or do, but as I look back on my life I see God's hand in it. I cannot even image doing anything else. The most precious place in this world that He has given us is to be focused and Christ-centered.

My heart's desire is to be in the place that God wants me to be—to glorify His son, Jesus Christ—and to honor Him with my life. I pray that as you hold this book in your hands, you can see a life that went from tragedy to triumph—but it took Christ dying on the Cross-for this soul to see what He had for me. He knew me before I ever took a breath in this world. I am so glad He has allowed me to know Him.

HIS SERVANT FOR LIFE!!!

Acknowledgements

I thank my Lord and Savior Jesus Christ. For a life now focused on the truth to helping others. Prayerfully, I will continue to listen to you each and every day of my life! Thank you for using a person like me!

I want to thank my precious husband Geoff Adams for loving me for the past 42 years. For encouraging me during the past 15 years in this ministry, with times of crying, laughing, times I wanted to quit my job and holding me when it was way to hard. Being my rock, when I started to stumble off the stones. Hearing me screaming, "I need help with my computer, ugh!" and trying to be so patient with me. Yes there were days, I wanted to throw my computer out the window, but you were there to rescue me again! Writing my life story was a big step for me and you are my biggest cheerleader! Thank you my honey, I love you very much! I thank God each day that He put you into my life!

To Geoffrey Jr and Michael Adams, my precious sons that I did give birth to. You both have prayed for your mom, encouraged me and are very excited to see what God is going to do with this book. Forgive me for not being the mom that you both needed when you were both younger. I knew there was something wrong with me, but could never figure it out, until later on in life. I was emotionally tied up with myself and wanted only to please me. Sometimes I wish I could go back in time and do it all over again and be the mom that you both deserved. I love you so much and hope I make you proud to be your mom! I am very proud of you both, my 2 wonderful sons!

To my precious daughter in law, Beth Adams (Michael's wife), for your encouragement, prayers, our crazy phone calls, your hugs and just listening to me when I was excited and frustrated. Thank you for all the times you said to me "Mom, it will be worth it, look at all the people you going to help." Thank you Beth, for being my friend, my daughter in love and just being a phone call away, I love you so much!

I also want to thank my precious grandchildren that prayed for me, even though they did not know about the book or certain things in my life, but knew that Grandma needed prayers. A lot of love and hugs and kisses to each one of you!!

To my friend, Vera Dormady thank you for praying with me, telling me "get going on this Pati." and sometimes saying, "Leave it." Being so excited about what is going to happen with this book! You are a special and loving friend, Thank you for being in my life! Love you!

Thank you Gail Zaichek for your strength, encouragement, and your love. Guiding me to stay the course and the goal I had. Telling me, God has great plans for me, and this book. I cannot tell you how blessed I am to have you in my life, Love you my friend!

Thank you Dennis Dormady, for helping me sort out my mess with the family pictures and reading my manuscript. You are amazing with the computer and thanks for taken my Author Picture!! 2 thumbs up!

To my editor, B.R. Fleury, what can I say!! Thanks for all the encouragement, all those funny words you would use, to get me thinking about how I worded things. It sure did help me! Thanks for all the time and hours you put into this for me and with me!!

To my friend, Meredith, thanks for your words of encouragement and praying for me. Thanks for all those Meredith hugs!!! Love you!

To my friend Teri McClelland, you're prayers, your love & encouragement. Love you!

Lisa Dudley Adams thanks for being a prayer partner in the Recovery part of this world. Thank you for being in the battle with me, oh yes, and all the phone calls we shared together. I know many more to come! This is an awesome journey God has us on and I love serving side by side with you. Love you!

Stacy Massey, for encouragement and prayers. God bless you and love ya!

My friend Becky Burnett, you and my former Sunday school class at FBC, I thank you for praying for me. Becky, you are a wonderful, generous, praying and caring friend. And oh, how I love your laugh and smile!! Love you!!

To Helen and Dale Chapman, for encouragement, prayers and support. Love you both.

To my friends, Patti Baudhuin Dines, Pat Vasil and Linda Maier, Grace Beezie, Carol Smith, Chris B. and Flo M. You all were the first ones to pray for me in this journey of writing this book back in 2001. Thanks so much my friends!! Love you all!

To my Executive Director friends in Connecticut, Lisa Maloney, Donnita Young & Linda Cochrane, for being there when I needed to talk, whether phone call or e-mail. You all are such a blessing to me! Thanks for all the prayers! God Bless you all!

To Richard H. and Gina H, Wow, what can I say, to two wonderful Godly people that have encouraged me, prayed with me. Gina thanks for all your words of encouragement with e-mails. Thanks for the guidance in all areas I might need to go to or people I need to work with. I thank you both from the bottom of my heart!

To the film producers and directors that I spoke with or e-mailed with, that gave me uplifting words and encouraged me to follow my dreams.

I thank God for all the clients that I have seen, counseled with in the past 15 years that have touched my life and my heart. Your tears and smiles were very real, your hugs were warm and genuine. You all have shown me so much and shared your life with me. So with a humble heart, I say thank you, to all of you that have walked down that road with me, I will never forget you.

To all the crisis pregnancy centers out there, in the battlefield, stay focused, stay strong, and stay the course God has for each of you. The enemy may win some battles, but God wins the war! You have a warrior with you, in me.

To all the Facilitators working with the Post Abortion Recovery Programs, stay faithful, stay strong, stay the course. Be faithful to the calling that Jesus Christ has called you too.

I know there is a lot of people I could thank, but I would be writing for a very long time, so please forgive me. God has placed in my life, so many people to guide, direct me, encourage me and tell me what I am doing wrong or what I am doing right. This has been an amazing journey and I know its not over yet!

A Special Thank You

To Walt and Linda Wilbourne, for giving Geoff those tapes of Pastor Jim Holbrook's sermons. I just saw no reason for those tapes and really thought it would be a waste of time to listen to them. Out of the 5 or 6 tapes you gave him, I picked up the one God wanted me to hear. Thank you for your encouragement, prayers and being faithful servants of God. Thank you for inviting us to Church. Oh, not to mention the free breakfast we received too! God used both of you, for us to hear the truth.. Thank you from the bottom of my heart!

To Pastor Jim Holbrook, you are a faithful man of God and a wonderful Pastor. God has truly called you to preach the word of God! I really was not happy those tapes landed on Geoff's dresser, but one night, I just grabbed one, thinking, "what am I doing, I am not going to listen to this!" That night changed my life and I was never the same again. God removed the veil from my eyes that night. Pastor Holbrook, this humble heart thanks you for preaching the word of God, caring enough to visit us a few days later, to see how we were doing, to answer any questions we may have and to pray with us. Starting out as a new Christian, you showed us what it truly means to walk the walk and not just talk the talk. So again I say---- Thank-you!!

FORGIVENESS

Webster's Dictionary says:

To stop feeling anger toward (someone who has done something wrong): to stop blaming (someone). To stop feeling anger about (something): to forgive someone for (something wrong).

Other words would be, pardon, absolution, exoneration, remission, dispensation, reprieve and mercy.

The Bible says:

Ephesians-4: 32 "Be kind to one another, tender hearted, forgiving each other just as God in Christ also has forgiven you" (NKJ)

Colossians 3:13 "bearing with one another and forgiving one another, if anyone has a compliant against another even as Christ forgave you, so you also must do."
(NKJ)

Ephesians 1:7- "In Him we have redemption through His blood, the forgiveness of sins, according to the riches of His grace/" (NKJ)

Now that you have read my story, I indeed have truly forgiven people for the things that they did to me and I pray that they have forgiven me for the things I have done to them. Not to forgive people for things that they may have done to you or your family is to hold onto something that can destroy your life and is not pleasing to God. What good is this doing to your physical, mental and spiritual life? Not good at all. The stress, pain and anger creep in and before you know it, you are immersed in it. Each day I pray to be pleasing in His sight.

Referals/ Resources

If you have had an abortion & looking for help:

INTERNATIONAL HELPLINE FOR ABORTION RECOVERY & PREVENTION

866-482-LIFE (5433) www.internationalhelpline.org
24 /7
Confidential Help
Call and talk with trained phone consultants, who have experienced the pain of abortion, but have healed to help others.

ARIN- ABORTION RECOVERY INTERNATIONAL:

www.abortionrecovery.org
Click on Care Directory.

If you or someone you know are in a crisis pregnancy there is help:

www.pregnancydecisionline.org
Or Call 1-877-791-5475

www.optionline.org
Or Call 1-800-712-4357
Or Text- 313131

ON LINE FOR LIFE:

www.onlineforlife.org

Call—(888)-884-8160
They can direct you to a life—affirming pregnancy center, which will give you a pregnancy test, truth and one on one compassionate counseling.

To contact Pati Adams: www.patiadamsbytheseashore.com